Richard Holloway is a former Bishop of Edinburgh and Professor of Divinity at Gresham College. He is a Fellow of the Royal Society of Edinburgh, and a former Chairman of the Scottish Arts Council (2005–2010). His books include *Godless Morality*, *Doubts and Loves*, *Looking in the Distance* and *Leaving Alexandria*, which won a PEN/Ackerley Prize for autobiography.

HOW TO READ

How to Read Ancient Philosophy by Miriam Leonard
How to Read Aquinas by Timothy McDermott
How to Read Beauvoir by Stella Sandford
How to Read Darwin by Mark Ridley
How to Read Derrida by Penelope Deutscher
How to Read Descartes by John Cottingham
How to Read the Egyptian Book of the Dead by Barry Kemp
How to Read Foucault by Johanna Oksala
How to Read Freud by Josh Cohen
How to Read Heidegger by Mark Wrathall
How to Read Hitler by Neil Gregor
How to Read Hume by Simon Blackburn
How to Read Joyce by Derek Attridge
How to Read Jung by David Tacey
How to Read Kierkegaard by John D. Caputo
How to Read Lacan by Slavoj Žižek
How to Read Machiavelli by Maurizio Viroli
How to Read Marx by Peter Osborne
How to Read Montaigne by Terence Cave
How to Read Nietzsche by Keith Ansell Pearson
How to Read Plato by Richard Kraut
How to Read the Qur'an by Mona Siddiqui
How to Read Sade by John Phillips
How to Read Sartre by Robert Bernasconi
How to Read Shakespeare by Nicholas Royle
How to Read Wittgenstein by Ray Monk

THE GOOD BOOK

HOW TO READ THE BIBLE

RICHARD HOLLOWAY

GRANTA

I am grateful to Bella Lacey of Granta for encouraging me to write this book, and for her expert help in editing it.

Granta Publications, 12 Addison Avenue, London W11 4QR

First published in Great Britain as *How to Read the Bible*
by Granta Books 2006
This edition published by Granta Books 2014

A CIP catalogue record for this book is available from the British Library.

1 3 5 7 9 10 8 6 4 2

ISBN 978 1 78378 026 6
eISBN 978 1 78378 103 4

Typeset by M Rules

Printed and bound by CPI Group (UK) Ltd, Croydon, CR0 4YY

CONTENTS

How am I to read *How to Read*?

This series is based on a very simple, but novel idea. Most beginners' guides to great thinkers and writers offer either potted biographies or condensed summaries of their major works, or perhaps even both. *How to Read*, by contrast, brings the reader face-to-face with the writing itself in the company of an expert guide. Its starting point is that in order to get close to what a writer is all about, you have to get close to the words they actually use and be shown how to read those words.

Every book in the series is in a way a masterclass in reading. Each author has selected ten or so short extracts from a writer's work and looks at them in detail as a way of revealing their central ideas and thereby opening doors onto a whole world of thought. Sometimes these extracts are arranged chronologically to give a sense of a thinker's development over time, sometimes not. The books are not merely compilations of a thinker's most famous passages, their 'greatest hits', but rather they offer a series of clues or keys that will enable readers to go on and make discoveries of their own. In addition to the texts and readings, each book provides a short biographical chronology and suggestions for further reading, Internet resources, and so on. The books in the *How to Read* series don't claim to tell you all you need to know about Freud, Nietzsche and Darwin, or indeed Shakespeare and the Marquis de Sade, but they do offer the best starting point for further exploration.

Unlike the available second-hand versions of the minds that have shaped our intellectual, cultural, religious, political and scientific landscape, *How to Read* offers a refreshing set of first-hand encounters with those minds. Our hope is that these books will, by turn, instruct, intrigue, embolden, encourage and delight.

Simon Critchley
New School for Social Research, New York

INTRODUCTION

Advising people on how to read the Bible is a complex task. By one estimate, there are 66 books in the Protestant Bible, 73 books in the Roman Catholic Bible, 77 books in the Eastern Orthodox Bible and – unlike most other texts in this series – they are believed to be divinely inspired. Among Christians the Bible is held to be either the literally dictated word of God or to contain words inspired directly by God. If we ask on what authority these claims are made, we are told that the Bible itself makes them – and that's that. It is easy to mock this kind of circularity, and no one did it more scathingly than Matthew Tindal, an eighteenth-century divine: 'It's an odd jumble to prove the truth of a book by the truth of the doctrines it contains, and at the same time conclude these doctrines to be true because contained in that book.'[1] It is the hermetic circularity of religious argument that accounts for the frustration many feel when they encounter protagonists who argue a case not on its merits, but on the basis of the transcendental authority of the Bible. Interestingly, this is a frustration encountered among believers themselves, as the current debate in the Anglican Church over the moral status of homosexuals noisily demonstrates. Traditionalists, for whom the Bible is the sole authority for human behaviour, cite their texts and thereby deem the matter to be concluded; whereas liberals, who accord some authority to contemporary understandings of human nature, hold that the Bible should be a partner in a dialogue with humanity, not a dictator over it.

Equally contentious, though at the moment mainly confined to the USA, is the debate between Creationists and Evolutionists. On the basis of the self-authenticating authority of the Bible, Creationists assert that the world and its inhabitants were established in six days roughly seven thousand years ago. Evolutionists, convinced by the discoveries of Charles Darwin and his followers, assert that living species on earth emerged over an unimaginably long period of time by a process of experimental adaptation. Interestingly, there is a mediating position between the opposed protagonists, sometimes called Intelligent Design, which will provide us with an opening into one school of biblical interpretation. Believers in Intelligent Design agree with Creationists about the existence of an ultimate designer, but they think his method of operating was the one discovered by Darwin. For them the world is the way science describes it, except for the single claim that it is the work of God. The intriguing thing about this debate is that it shows that even within the community of believers there are different ways of reading the Bible. Some devout interpreters give it an absolute supra-historical authority. If you read the Bible from their perspective, it locks you permanently into the world view of texts that reached their final form 2000 years ago. We only have to think about the revolution that has occurred in the status of women to see how difficult it must be to maintain this kind of belief in the authority of the Bible, while respecting society's current ethical imperatives. That is why a more subtle and flexible approach to scripture emerged among liberal thinkers within the believing community. For them, all history, including the history of the Bible, is a gradual process of divine disclosure that is commensurate with human rationality and its discoveries. Applying this principle to the Bible means you can accept an entirely naturalistic account of its history, but with the significant proviso that its ultimate, originating authority is God. Like the world, the Bible is seen as the work of God, but its nature and meaning are disclosed to us by the steady application of the tools of historical and scientific research rather than by simply pressing the PRINT key on a sacred computer. That is why, while some Christians prefer to read the Bible in a straight literalistic way, others come at its meaning more circuitously: it just depends on what kind of believer they are.

Is reading the Bible, then, a sport for believers only, whether traditionalist or liberal, or can anyone get into the game? The answer ought to be a resounding 'yes': not only can you get into the game, you ought to get into it, because it is too important to leave to believers. To justify that claim, let me offer a triangulation approach to biblical interpretation. Just as a triangle has three angles, so there are three ways of reading the Bible: two for believers, and one for unbelievers. I have already covered the views from the believing base of the triangle: the angle from the right that takes the Bible as literal dictation from God; and the angle from the left that takes it as a completely human construct, though prompted by God, whose will can be discerned by means of an intelligent interpretation of it. Though they come to very different conclusions about it, both of these readings accord extrinsic authority to the Bible – its value finally comes from outside itself.

Let us look now at the third angle of our triangle, and bring in the ancient Greeks to assist us. The Greeks employed an interesting distinction in their use of language. They used the word *logos* for factual discourse about things you could verify through the senses. But they used the word *muthos* to describe another kind of meaning. The most characteristic use of this word was to classify stories about the gods, which is why it is easily misunderstood today. The word 'myth' has become synonymous with something false or untrue, like the existence of those old Greek gods. Yet the question we should ask of a myth is not whether it is true or false, but whether it is living or dead, and whether it still carries meaning for us today. When Sigmund Freud was exploring the mysteries of human nature, he borrowed the language of Greek mythology to express his discoveries. Take his theory of what he calls the Oedipus complex.[2] In the Greek myth Oedipus was the son of the King and Queen of Thebes. To avert the prophecy that he would one day kill his father and marry his mother, he was exposed on the mountains as an infant. Rescued and reared by shepherds, and unaware of his lineage, when he grew to manhood Oedipus unwittingly killed his father and married his mother. Freud uses this myth to explain what he called the Oedipus complex, the psycho-analytic term for a son's unacknowledged sexual desire for his mother and hatred of his father.

As well as adapting Greek myth to his own purposes, Freud was a bit of a myth-maker himself, as his theory of the mind demonstrates. He gave it three interacting levels: there was what he called the *id*, an unconscious reservoir of impulsive needs and instincts; then there was the *super-ego*, which was formed by the pressures and prohibitions of parents and society as a censor and controller of the undisciplined urges of the *id*; and living between the two is the poor old *ego*, the conscious mind, the bit we are most aware of, though we are usually ignorant of the pressures upon it of its noisy siblings. Now we know that our minds don't come in literal layers like a three-storey car park, with the *id* in the basement, the *ego* at

ground level, and the *super-ego* up the stairs on th
but Freud's myth does correspond to the way we
life. We have overpowering desires that are often
control with our rational minds, so we sometimes overcorrect
them and end as uptight, repressed personalities. What Freud
gives us is neither hard science nor a factually exact map of the
human psyche; it is metaphor; it is myth: that is why when we
read him we grasp the truth of his insights experientially
rather than theoretically. As with the old myths, much of
what he writes corresponds to the way we encounter the
tumult of our own minds. That is why he is better understood
as a therapeutic artist or priest than as a scientist; and it is why
he is often wilfully misunderstood by rigorously empirical
thinkers. And that is what has happened to the Bible as well:
unimaginative literalists have destroyed its reputation by insist-
ing on the factual truth of the myth of the Fall in Genesis
rather than encouraging us to read it as a metaphor for the
enduring human capacity for self-destruction. This is where
Freud's approach can help us. Reading the Bible through the
lens of myth can be illuminating, even for unbelievers. For
readers who follow this approach the Bible has intrinsic not
extrinsic authority; it carries the power of its meaning within
itself, like any great text. It is significant that the community
that is most aware of the power of sacred texts to help humanity in its search for well-being is the psychotherapeutic
profession. Susie Orbach has said that she admires theologians who work their material in a therapeutic way. This is
what religious practitioners at their best have always done.
They have used their narratives to help us understand ourselves, and change for the better. Though this is the way of
reading the Bible I shall commend in this book, it need not be
discontinuous with the interpretation offered by believers.

Just as believers can accept the way science sees the world, though they believe God is its final cause, so they can accept the way philosophy reads the Bible, though they believe God is its final author. For the purposes of such a person-centred approach to biblical interpretation, therefore, we can agree with Norman MacCaig when he says that 'God, like me, is an atheist.'[3] Whether or not we believe in God, we can leave him to one side when we read the good book, because the best of it carries its own meaning within itself: in other words, its authority is intrinsic. That is the angle I will be coming from; but before diving into the text, let me offer some facts about the body of material we will be dealing with. Non-anoraks may, if they prefer, skip the next section and jump immediately to Chapter 1.

HOW MANY PARTS?

A fact that I have already noted – that the Bible comes in different sizes for the different Christian traditions – should alert us to an ancient dispute about which texts qualify for entry. For Protestant Christians the Bible comes in only two parts, the Old and New Testaments. These are loaded words, of course, the assumption behind them being that the Old Testament, strictly speaking the Hebrew Bible, has been superseded or fulfilled by the New Testament: which is precisely what Christians officially believe. When, towards the end of the first century of the Christian Era, the followers of Jesus finally broke away from the Jewish community, they took the family jewels with them, claiming that God had rejected the people of the old covenant or testament for refusing to recognize Jesus as the Messiah. As the Gospel of John put it at the time: 'He came to his own home, and his own people received him not.'[4] So God adopted a new people, who inherited the vocation of old Israel. Even Paul, who provides us with the most systematic version of this claim, had qualms about it and suggests that it was a ruse on God's part to make the old Israel jealous and rush back into his arms.[5] Today, Christians are increasingly sensitive to this brand of theological imperialism and talk not of Old and New Testaments, but of the Hebrew Bible and the Christian Bible: but any Christian Bible you pick up will describe itself defiantly as *The Holy Bible, containing the Old and New Testaments.* In this book I shall respect both traditions by mixing the usage: I shall refer to what Christians call the Old Testament as the Hebrew Bible, but I shall refer to the explicitly Christian section as the New Testament.

However, some Bibles have a third section and describe themselves as, 'The Holy Bible, containing the Old and New Testaments *and Apocrypha*', or 'The Holy Bible, containing the Old and New Testaments *with the Apocrypha*', which is why we find Bibles of different sizes among Christians. To understand the status of this third level of material it will help if we return to the idea of the two testaments. The Hebrew Bible was established in its final form somewhere between 200 BCE and the birth of Jesus. Though the New Testament was not canonically established by the Church till the Council of Constantinople in 397, the texts in it were probably all written by the year 100 of the Christian Era. The third set of texts, called the Apocrypha (from the Greek word for 'secret' or 'hidden') was composed between 200 before the Christian Era (BCE) and year 100 of the Christian Era (CE). Though these books are not found in the canonical Hebrew Bible, they were included in a famous Greek translation of it called the

Septuagint, which is how they found their way into some versions of the Christian Bible. Their inclusion has been disputed on the grounds enunciated by St Jerome, when writing his famous Latin translation of the Bible, that they lacked proper authority because they were written in Greek not Hebrew. That is why they are sometimes described as deutero-canonical, secondary works of a later date. Though you won't usually find them in old Protestant Bibles, they are found in most of the modern translations of the Bible, such as the Revised English Bible, the Revised Standard Version, or the New Revised Standard Version. Incidentally, it is the NRSV I have used in this book for two reasons: the comparative accuracy of the translation, and because it is likely to be more accessible to new students than some of the more traditional translations.

DOCUMENTARY HYPOTHESES

Most scholars believe that some of the most significant texts in the Hebrew and Christian scriptures were radically edited into their present shape from material that had its origin in other forms. For example, the books of Genesis, Exodus and Numbers were rigorously examined by scholars in the nineteenth century and various hypotheses about their composition were offered. On the basis of different versions of the same story, the use of different names for the same place, and different names for God, it was suggested that a variety of sources had been redacted into a single text. This theory was called the documentary hypothesis, and it has had various forms ever since, all of which points to the difficulty of speaking with absolute accuracy about how the Bible was formed.

However, Robert Alter, one of the most distinguished Hebrew scholars writing today, is distinctly unimpressed by the claims that are sometimes made on behalf of the documentary hypotheses. He says that all the details of the documentary approach are continually, and often quite vehemently debated.[6] Of his own translation of Genesis he writes: 'One need not say that Genesis is a unitary artwork, like, say, a novel by Henry James, in order to grant it integrity as a book. There are other instances of works of art that evolve over the centuries, like the cathedrals of medieval Europe, and are the product of many hands, involving an elaborate process of editing, like some of the greatest Hollywood films.'[7] The idea of understanding the Bible as a composition like a medieval cathedral, or even a Hollywood blockbuster, is appealing and worth remembering when we start dipping into the text.

Though the Christian end of the Bible is a much later addition to the rambling old cathedral, it raises a similar problem. The most celebrated version of a documentary hypothesis as applied to the New Testament concerns the gospels of Matthew, Mark and Luke. They are called the *synoptics* because they have a similar point of view on Jesus, unlike John, who comes at him from a different angle. The most commonly held view of the synoptic gospels is that Matthew and Luke are later compositions than Mark, whom they both incorporate into their own text. In addition to Mark, they each had access to a body of sayings which scholars call Q, from the German *Quelle* for source. And they each had an independent body of material used only by them, labelled M and L.

The enduring existence of these theories or hypotheses should alert modern readers of the Bible to the fact that they are dealing with complex material, most of it anonymous, much of which probably started its life in the oral tradition that was such a powerful part of the culture of ancient societies. But the current state of play in these scholarly competitions need not concern the general reader, who can engage with the Bible as a finished text, however arrived at, that carries its own meaning independent of its exact origin.

DODGY ATTRIBUTIONS

It is worth spending a minute alerting the reader to the fact that the authorship of ancient texts is frequently attributed to famous names who had little or nothing to do with them. The most famous case of dodgy attribution is the ancient tradition that Moses wrote the first five books of the Hebrew Bible, Genesis, Exodus, Leviticus, Numbers and Deuteronomy, collectively described as the Pentateuch, and of unique significance to Judaism. Open your Bible at the beginning and it announces 'The First Book of Moses, commonly called Genesis'. In *The Complete Bible Handbook* John Bowker carefully notes that some passages are unlikely to have been written by Moses, such as the account of his own death in Deuteronomy 34 or the claim in Numbers 12 that he was the most humble man who ever lived.[8]

But the dodgiest attributions are probably found in the New Testament, where the intent was to give authority to the item in question by associating it with one of the apostles. The most egregious example of a mistaken attribution in the New Testament is the Epistle to the Hebrews, which the King James Version announces as having been written by Paul the Apostle. It is significant that my New Revised Standard

Version simply announces it as The Letter to the Hebrews. Most scholars today have no idea who wrote it, but they are certain it was not Paul. One of them, the distinguished Catholic New Testament scholar Raymond Brown, says that the evidence against Paul's having written Hebrews is overwhelming.[9] And that is enough for me. There are other, less blatant, misattributions in the New Testament, including I and II Timothy and Titus, almost certainly not written by Paul, though they may contain Pauline fragments, which is why they are sometimes described as deutero-Pauline, to bring in that useful qualifier again. But since this book does not believe that authorship of itself adds value to the authority of a biblical text, readers need not concern themselves with the issue, unless they enjoy literary detective work, in which case a whole new field of endeavour tantalizingly opens before them.

AUTHENTICITY

The real heat in the issue of authenticity concerns the four books called gospels in the New Testament. Did Jesus say, for instance, as the Gospel of John has it: 'I am the way, and the truth, and the life; no one comes to the Father, but by me',[10] thereby declaring, in effect, that the only way to God was through Christianity? Questions of the authenticity of such sayings can have powerful negative and positive effects. Secular-minded unbelievers, who might benefit from thinking about the impact and significance of Jesus, are likely to be put off by the extravagant personal claims that issue from his mouth in the gospels, particularly in John. Sayings such as, 'He that has seen me has seen the Father' or 'I and the Father are one' or 'Before Abraham was, I am'[11] can really only be understood as claims to divine status on the part of Jesus: but who could trust a man who thought he was God? On the other hand, this is precisely the positive meaning many Christians put on the words: they are a challenge to humanity by Jesus, the God–Man, and they bring us all to a moment of decision. But the heat is taken out of the claim, negatively as well as positively, if Jesus didn't actually say the words, if they are not, in fact, authentic. This brings us to the heart of the hottest debate in New Testament studies: how many of the sayings attributed to Jesus are authentic, and by what tests can we determine the matter? Most scholars detect four strands of material in the gospels, on a sliding scale of authenticity. One influential group of radical New Testament scholars in the USA, the Jesus Seminar, actually uses a colour-coded voting system when authenticating texts. When they vote on a text they ask their members to drop a coloured bead into a box according to the following system:

a red bead means: Jesus undoubtedly said this or something very like it;

a pink bead means: Jesus probably said something like this;

a grey bead means: Jesus did not say this, but the ideas contained in it are close to his own;

a black bead means: Jesus did not say this; it represents the perspective or content of a later or different tradition.[12]

If you comb through the translation these scholars made of the first three gospels you see a pattern of red, pink and grey on every page, against a predominant background of black; but when you turn to their translation of the fourth gospel, the one attributed to John, the text is an unrelieved black. This verdict on the inauthenticity of John reflects a significant consensus among many, though far from all, scholars that the fourth gospel is a creation of the early church and represents a significant theological development in the Christian understanding of the status of Jesus. In other words, though Jesus did not claim to be divine, his followers made the claim on his behalf, after years of meditation on his continuing impact on their lives. Obviously, these are deep theological waters into which few amateurs will wish to plunge, but they should alert readers to the developmental complexities of the New Testament. Some of these issues will surface in the chapters that follow in this book.

BEGINNING

Genesis [1:1,2; 2:7–9, 18, 21–5]
In the beginning when God created the heavens and the earth, [2] the earth was a formless void and darkness covered the face of the deep, while a wind from God swept over the face of the waters . . .

[2:7] then the Lord God formed man from the dust of the ground, and breathed into his nostrils the breath of life; and the man became a living being. [8] And the Lord God planted a garden in Eden, in the east; and there he put the man whom he had formed. [9] Out of the ground the Lord God made to grow every tree that is pleasant to the sight and good for food, the tree of life also in the midst of the garden, and the tree of the knowledge of good and evil . . .

[18] Then the Lord God said, 'It is not good that the man should be alone; I will make him a helper as his partner.' . . . [21] So the Lord God caused a deep sleep to fall upon the man, and he slept; then he took one of his ribs and closed up its place with flesh. [22] And the rib that the Lord God had taken from the man he made into a woman and brought her to the man. [23] Then the man said,

'This at last is bone of my bones
   and flesh of my flesh;
this one shall be called Woman,
   for out of Man this one was taken.'

[24] Therefore a man leaves his father and his mother and clings to his wife, and they become one flesh. [25] And the man and his wife were both naked, and were not ashamed.

God is the dominant character in the Bible: he walks on stage at the beginning and stays there, though he goes offstage for a break from time to time — for instance, he doesn't feature at all in the Book of Esther. To read the Bible profitably, therefore, you have to work out what your line on God is going to be and, if possible, stick to it throughout. Two approaches to God have the beauty of simplicity, and they are not as mutually contradictory as they might at first appear. The traditional view is that he is the supreme reality who existed before the universe, which he created, and which he sustains in being by his will. The other attractively simple approach is to see God not as the one who created us, but as the one created by us to explain our own existence. If you read the Bible from this angle, God is the way we talk about the mysteries of our own nature, so our interrogation of the Bible is a form of self-analysis. However, the two approaches are not necessarily as incongruent with each other as they might at first appear. If you believe God is real, then the commandments he gave to Moses have authority over us because they are his prescription for the moral life of humanity. On the other hand, if you believe God is a human invention, then so are the ten commandments, so it follows that any authority they have over us comes from our own struggles to organize ourselves into harmonious communities. The trouble with all thinking about God is that it is an unavoidably human process, and one of the things we know about ourselves is that we inescapably project something of ourselves onto whatever we think about. Or, to use another metaphor, everything we encounter is filtered through the lens of our own complex selfhood, with inevitably distorting results. Now, if we constantly distort the reality of other people, whom we *have* seen, we can be doubly sure that we are bound to distort the reality of God, whom no one has ever seen.[13] That is why it is wise of those who believe in a real God to recognize that he can only come to them filtered through the lens of their own fallible humanity, so they should be modest and wary in the claims they make about him. As a matter of fact, one of the constant themes in the Bible is precisely the human capacity to get God wrong, which is why the distance between those who believe God is a human invention and those who believe God is real is narrower than we might think. Maybe that is why the God of the Bible often seems to be less concerned with those who deny his existence than with those who confidently claim to know what he is up to.

Whichever way you look at it, therefore, we can honestly say that from the beginning we have been thinking about God, and whether real or a human invention, what we say about him tells us a lot about ourselves. That's why a careful reading of the Bible can be revelatory, though not necessarily in the way claimed by religion's official exponents. Whether the Bible does reveal inside information about the nature of a real god will remain forever debatable: what is beyond debate is that it reveals inside information about the nature of humanity. That is why it is still worth reading. One of the things the opening chapters of the Bible tell us about ourselves is that, frail bipeds though we are, our minds are extraordinarily fertile, and from them whole universes are born. But they also remind us how easy it is for us to make wrong choices, and in doing so sabotage our own happiness.

[3:1] Now the serpent was more crafty than any other wild animal that the Lord God had made. He said to the woman, 'Did God say, "You shall not eat from any tree in the garden"?' [2] The woman said to the serpent, 'We may eat of the fruit of the trees in the garden; [3] but God said, "You shall not eat of the fruit of the tree that is in the middle of the garden, nor shall you touch it, or you shall die."' [4] But the serpent said to the woman, 'You will not die; [5] for God knows that when you eat of it your eyes will be opened, and you will be like God, knowing good and evil.' [6] So when the woman saw that the tree was good for food, and that it was a delight to the eyes, and that the tree was to be desired to make one wise, she took of its fruit and ate; and she also gave some to her husband, who was with her, and he ate. [7] Then the eyes of both were opened, and they knew that they were naked; and they sewed fig leaves together and made loincloths for themselves.

[8] They heard the sound of the Lord God walking in the garden at the time of the evening breeze, and the man and his wife hid themselves from the presence of the Lord God among the trees of the garden. [9] But the Lord God called to the man, and said to him, 'Where are you?' [10] He said, 'I heard the sound of you in the garden, and I was afraid, because I was naked; and I hid myself.' [11] He said, 'Who told you that you were naked? Have you eaten from the tree of which I commanded you not to eat?' [12] The man said, 'The woman whom you gave to be with me, she gave me fruit from the tree, and I ate.' [13] Then the Lord God said to the woman, 'What is this that you have done?' The woman said, 'The serpent tricked me, and I ate.' [14] The Lord God said to the serpent,

'Because you have done this,
    cursed are you among all animals
    and among all wild creatures;
upon your belly you shall go,
    and dust you shall eat
    all the days of your life.
[15] I will put enmity between you and the woman,
    and between your offspring and hers;
he will strike your head,
    and you will strike his heel.'
[16] To the woman he said,
    'I will greatly increase your pangs in childbearing;
    in pain you shall bring forth children,
yet your desire shall be for your husband,
    and he shall rule over you.'
[17] And to the man he said,
    'Because you have listened to the voice of your wife,

and have eaten of the tree
about which I commanded you,
    "You shall not eat of it",
cursed is the ground because of you;
    in toil you shall eat of it all the days of your life;
[18] thorns and thistles it shall bring forth for you;
    and you shall eat the plants of the field.
[19] By the sweat of your face
    you shall eat bread
until you return to the ground,
    for out of it you were taken;
you are dust,
    and to dust you shall return.'
  [20] The man named his wife Eve, because she was the mother of
all living. [21] And the Lord God made garments of skins for the man
and for his wife, and clothed them.
  [22] Then the Lord God said, 'See, the man has become like one
of us, knowing good and evil; and now, he might reach out his hand
and take also from the tree of life, and eat, and live for ever' – [23]
therefore the Lord God sent him forth from the garden of Eden, to till
the ground from which he was taken. [24] He drove out the man; and
at the east of the garden of Eden he placed the cherubim, and a
sword flaming and turning to guard the way to the tree of life.

It is no exaggeration to describe this ancient myth as the most
fateful fiction in human history, but to sustain the claim we
have to fast forward thousands of years to Paul's Letter to the
Romans. Paul was the principal architect of the Christian doctrinal system, and his use of this story alerts us to the dangers
of some ways of reading the Bible. It also reminds us that the
afterlife of great texts eclipses the intention of the original
author, even if we think we know what it was. Unlike a lot of
literary warfare, disputes about the Bible have consequences for
the actual lives of real human beings. In the introduction I
mentioned an ancient distinction in human discourse: there
was logos, a factual narrative about actual events; and there was

muthos, a fictional narrative that yet carried profound truth. I ought to add here that we make more of the distinction today than the ancients did, for a very obvious reason. Though we can't be certain, it is likely that back then *muthoi* were also thought of as *logoi*; so the pre-modern mind may have understood the narrative of the Fall as a historical account of a primordial catastrophe, as well as a parable of the human condition. That is certainly how Paul read it, with profound consequences for human history. Here he is on the subject, in his Letter to the Romans: '[5:18] . . . just as one man's trespass led to condemnation for all, so one man's act of righteousness leads to justification and life for all. [19] For just as by the one man's disobedience the many were made sinners, so by the one man's obedience the many will be made righteous.'

Paul's reading of the myth of the Fall introduced a number of potent ideas into history that continue to reverberate. The most momentous was that Adam's disobedience passed guilt, like an indelible and incurable virus, onto the human race. This is a dramatic example not of exegesis, reading from the text, but of eisegesis, reading into the text, from the Greek verb meaning to 'lead' or 'bring into'. Retrojecting ideas from a later perspective into the text of the Hebrew Bible became a major enterprise in Christianity, with two branches, historical and theological. Historical eisegesis saw events in Christian history prefigured in the Hebrew scriptures, through which God secretly but intentionally foretold them. Some modern scholars claim that some of these events were actually manufactured to fulfil ancient prophecy, which is why one writer has described much of the New Testament not as history remembered but as prophecy historicized.[14] Though the extent of historical eisegesis in the New Testament is a matter mainly for scholarly debate, theological eisegesis has definitely had profound practical effects on actual lives. When Paul read the cause of his own obsessive moral struggles back into the myth of the Fall he grounded it in a forensic rather than a psychological understanding of the text. There is no suggestion in Genesis itself that the original author understood it in this way; and the Jews, whose story it is, after all, certainly never extrapolated universal human guilt from it.

Fatefully, Paul did, and it brings us to an important distinction. It is valid to read from the story of the Fall what theologians call *original sin*, the idea that humans, as a matter of observable fact, constantly make wrong choices and are afflicted with discontents that propel them from Edenic happiness into misery: but that is not remotely the same thing as the idea that we are born guilty of an offence that originated with our forebears. It is this notion of original guilt that lies at the base of what Christian theologians call the economy of salvation or redemption system. The doctrine can be expressed in various ways, but it usually goes something like this. Because their primordial ancestor committed the original sin, in God's eyes humans are born guilty. And because they have been utterly corrupted by Adam's curse, they are themselves incapable of purging their guilt by any act of reparation. So God provided a human who was uncorrupted by the original offence to purge it on our behalf. Here the thinking can go in different directions. One way says that Jesus did not have an earthly father, therefore he was born immune to original guilt, remembering that in ancient thought the woman was not believed to contribute any DNA to her children: she was merely the passive receptacle in which the man's seed germinated. Another approach, theologically more subtle, held that God sent his own son to recapitulate the history of early man, the difference being that this time the new

Adam obeyed the divine command. However we describe the role of Jesus in the transaction, the doctrine has had a profound impact on human self-understanding in the West, and built an enormous entail of guilt and depression into our psyche – which, incidentally, also serves to emphasize the colossal power our myths have over us. Paul's theory of original guilt was the engine that propelled the expansion of Christianity as a mission of rescue to a perishing world. If we do a rough calculation of the massive and continuing impact of Christian theology on humanity, it is clear that the anonymous author of this ancient myth was one of the most influential figures in history.

There is another element in the story that has had profound consequences in human history: its impact on women. The myth of the Fall provides us with the first example of man blaming woman for his own moral frailty: 'The woman whom you gave to be with me, she gave me fruit from the tree, and I ate.' Unfortunately, this is more than an early cartoon of the war of the sexes: it has had a profound negative impact on the actual lives of women. In its developed theological form it identified women as objects of temptation, designed to lure men to destruction, a device employed by witch-hunters in the past and counsel for the defence in rape cases today. Though it is difficult not to see in the Genesis story of the Fall some kind of reference to the problematic nature of human sexuality, in the Christian use of the story sex was additionally burdened with a heavier meaning, as the instrument whereby the virus of original guilt was passed down the generations. However you look at it, women were understood to be at the root of the male predicament: and they got the blame.

The problematic status of females in Christianity has had

some fascinating reverberations in later ecclesiastical history, none more intriguing than the dogma of the Immaculate Conception of the Virgin Mary promulgated by Pope Pius IX on 8 December 1854, which asserted that 'from the first moment of her conception the Blessed Virgin Mary was, by the singular grace and privilege of Almighty God, and in view of the merits of Jesus Christ, Saviour of mankind, kept free from all stain of original sin.'[15] The doctrine of the Immaculate Conception of Mary is not to be confused with the doctrine of the Virgin Birth of Jesus; but, once you accept the premise of the reality of original sin and its concomitant guilt, there is an exotic link between them. In this theological context, the purpose behind the idea of the Virgin Birth of Jesus is to show that, since he did not have a human father, he was born sinless, free of original guilt. The purpose behind the idea of the Immaculate Conception of Mary is to show that, though she had a human father, God miraculously intervened at the moment of her conception and blocked the transmission of original sin, presumably because he had already identified her as the maternal vehicle for the birth of his own son. These theological developments are more than the florid imaginings they might at first appear: they have had solid practical effects in human history. Indeed, just as Jesus was identified by Paul as the second Adam, so later Christian thinking identified Mary as the second Eve, and laid particular emphasis on her perpetual virginity. Here at last was a woman men could respect, one in whom motherhood was utterly separated from sexuality. It is this doctrine that lay at the root of the theology and sexual politics of Pope John Paul II, who died in 2005,[16] for 27 years leader of the world's billion Roman Catholics; so it could be argued that, far from being a piece of colourful theological exotica, it has had a profound impact on the lives of millions of women of our own day. We have come a long way from that apparently art-less little story in Genesis. If our interpretation of it has taught us anything, it surely has to be that how we read the Bible still matters, and matters profoundly.

2

PROMISING

Exodus [3:1] Moses was keeping the flock of his father-in-law Jethro, the priest of Midian; he led his flock beyond the wilderness, and came to Horeb, the mountain of God. [2] There the angel of the Lord appeared to him in a flame of fire out of a bush; he looked, and the bush was blazing, yet it was not consumed. [3] Then Moses said, 'I must turn aside and look at this great sight, and see why the bush is not burned up.' [4] When the Lord saw that he had turned aside to see, God called to him out of the bush, 'Moses, Moses!' And he said, 'Here I am.' [5] Then he said, 'Come no closer! Remove the sandals from your feet, for the place on which you are standing is holy ground.' [6] He said further, 'I am the God of your father, the God of Abraham, the God of Isaac, and the God of Jacob.' And Moses hid his face, for he was afraid to look at God.

[7] Then the Lord said, 'I have observed the misery of my people who are in Egypt; I have heard their cry on account of their taskmasters. Indeed, I know their sufferings, [8] and I have come down to deliver them from the Egyptians, and to bring them up out of that land to a good and broad land, a land flowing with milk and honey, to the country of the Canaanites, the Hittites, the Amorites, the Perizzites, the Hivites, and the Jebusites. [9] The cry of the Israelites has now come to me; I have also seen how the Egyptians oppress them. [10] So come, I will send you to Pharaoh to bring my people, the Israelites, out of Egypt.' [11] But Moses said to God, 'Who am I that I should go to Pharaoh, and bring the Israelites out of Egypt?' [12] He said, 'I will be with you; and this shall be the sign for you

that it is I who sent you: when you have brought the people out of Egypt, you shall worship God on this mountain.'

[13] But Moses said to God, 'If I come to the Israelites and say to them, "The God of your ancestors has sent me to you", and they ask me, "What is his name?" what shall I say to them?' [14] God said to Moses, 'I am who I am.' He said further, 'Thus you shall say to the Israelites, "I am has sent me to you."' [15] God also said to Moses, 'Thus you shall say to the Israelites, "The Lord, the God of your ancestors, the God of Abraham, the God of Isaac, and the God of Jacob, has sent me to you":

This is my name for ever,

and this my title for all generations.

[16] Go and assemble the elders of Israel, and say to them, "The Lord, the God of your ancestors, the God of Abraham, of Isaac, and of Jacob, has appeared to me, saying: I have given heed to you and to what has been done to you in Egypt. [17] I declare that I will bring you up out of the misery of Egypt, to the land of the Canaanites, the Hittites, the Amorites, the Perizzites, the Hivites, and the Jebusites, a land flowing with milk and honey."'

When we move from Genesis to Exodus, the second book of the Bible, we travel from the stubborn shadows of prehistory into the morning mists of real time, or something like it. I have put it vaguely like that, because it is by no means certain that we are dealing here with factual as opposed to theological history. Readers will not be surprised to encounter a text, like the one above, that wonders if God is real, because God is a notoriously elusive case; but what are they to think when they hear that Moses might not have been real either, nor even the great King David? The important thing to do, first of all, is to ask about the *use* we are making of the Bible and what it is we are expecting to get from our reading of it. So let me flip the question back at the puzzled reader and inquire: 'If you were to discover that the exodus of the children of Israel happened not in real history, but only in the pages of the Bible, what difference would it make to the power of the story?' My answer would be, 'It depends what you are using it for.' If you passionately believe that a real God called a real people from real slavery in a real Egypt and gave them eternal rights over a disputed stretch of real estate on a strip of land on the eastern Mediterranean, then it will obviously have profound practical effects on a number of issues, including who has rights to that particular piece of real estate today. But if you are reading these texts as mythic archetypes that express enduring themes in human history, then you will use them in a very different way. As I have already pointed out, it is just possible to merge both approaches, and to believe that, though there may be real history behind the narrative of Exodus, for us it is best used not to prove or disprove ancient claims, but to dramatize and illuminate present circumstances.

I think that is the best way to read the Bible today; but before moving on let me offer a nod in the direction of what the dispute is about. Biblical scholars of both the Hebrew Bible and the New Testament cover a very broad continuum from conservative to radical, going from a positive estimate of the historical reliability of the texts right over to those who believe there is hardly any history in them at all, except theological history.[17] As far as Exodus and the story of Moses goes, radical scholars would understand these texts as pure myth, constructed to provide a heroic and divinely inspired pedigree for a small clan wandering round the edges of the Syrian Empire.[18] While there may be remnants of genuine oral history lurking behind the texts, the texts themselves were composed a thousand years after the events they purport to describe, so we have no access to the events themselves. What is accessible to us is the use of the texts in interpreting

our own situation today. We can either use them as faith documents that give divine authority to a particular reading of
history, or as legends that express the struggles of the human
psyche, in which case they become hugely productive of
wisdom and insight. And in Exodus, four great and enduring
themes begin to emerge.

God is the dominant theme, and the second book of the
Bible takes a significant step in human thinking about the
divine. The God of Genesis is a naïve construct: he walks in
the garden of Eden in the cool of the day, very much like a
man just home from work before going indoors for his first
whisky of the evening. In Exodus this naïve primitivism disappears, and God becomes essentially invisible. From now on
his presence will be mediated, never direct; it will be
expressed sacramentally; the invisible and inaudible mystery of
God will manifest itself through, though it will never be contained by, that which is visible and audible – such as a thorn
bush in the wilderness. A Yiddish poem by Melech Ravitch,
translated by Ruth Whitman, captures the agonistic struggle
between the great Hebrew hero and the God who offered the
Israelites the dubious privilege of a special relationship:

What's going to be the end for both of us – God?
Are you really going to let me die like this
and really not tell me the big secret?

Must I really become dust, grey dust, and ash, black ash,
while the secret, which is closer than my shirt, than my skin,
still remains secret, though it's deeper in me than my own heart?

And was it really in vain that I hoped by day and waited by night?
And will you, until the very last moment, remain godlike-cruel and
      hard?
Your face deaf like dumb stone, like cement, blind-stubborn?

> Not for nothing is one of your thousand names – thorn, you thorn in
>   my spirit and flesh and bone,
> piercing me – I can't tear you out; burning me – I can't stamp you
>   out,
> moment I can't forget, eternity I can't comprehend.[19]

Ravitch called his poem 'Twelve Lines About the Burning Bush', and behind it is an ancient rabbinical tradition that the burning bush was a thorn bush. For Ravitch, God's elusiveness pierces like a thorn and burns like a fire – 'piercing me – I can't tear you out; burning me – I can't stamp you out'. The obsession with the reality or unreality of God does not pierce everyone, of course, but for those who feel the bite of the thorn or the burn of the flame, it does suggest the anguish of the search for the meaning or unmeaning of things in a universe that does not explain itself. The philosopher John Gray has an interesting response to this ancient and apparently incurable condition: he sees it as the product of the crystallization of language in writing. He claims that the calls of birds and the traces left by wolves to mark off their territories are no less forms of language than the words of humans. It was the invention of writing that proved to be the fateful development for humans, because it established an artificial memory that enabled them to enlarge their experience beyond the limits of one generation. The inevitable next step was the invention of a world of abstract entities that were mistaken for reality.[20] We don't have to accept Gray's theory of the original sin of writing to recognize that humans have a capacity for generating powerful abstractions that often turn back upon their creators and wreak terrible revenge upon them. The history of religious and ideological warfare is proof enough of the claim. Is this what God is? Have we projected our burning need for meaning onto an object we call God, and now divide ourselves into those who believe God is 'real' and those who don't?

What is intriguing about Moses' encounter with the God who spoke through the agency of the burning bush is that it provides us with a path that could lead us away from the predicament our abstractions have created for us; and it brings us to our second theme. When Moses asks the voice for its name it replies: *Ehyeh-Asher-Ehyeh*. Look up any commentary, or the footnotes in any annotated Bible, and you will be told that the meaning of these Hebrew words is uncertain; that they could be translated in various ways; and that they are all associated with the root *hayah*, 'to be'. Professor Alter says that the most plausible structure of the Hebrew is *I-Will-Be-Who-I-Will-Be*,[21] though it could be translated as *I Will Be What I Will Be* or *I Am Who I Am* or *I Am What I Am*. This is consonant with a powerful theme that gradually emerges in the Hebrew Bible, and is present also in the New Testament, which declares that God is an imperative voice calling us to a particular kind of action, not an object calling us to a particular kind of belief. In other words, it is not what you believe, but how you act that matters. But what happens if, like Paul, you find you are unable to live up to the standard set by that devouring voice? It is the uncompromising nature of the moral challenge in the Hebrew Bible that, paradoxically, lies at the root of Paul's great inversion of Christianity from an ethical into a theological religion, from a kind of practice into a kind of belief. Paul expresses the personal turmoil that lies at the root of his theological system in a famous passage in Romans.

Romans [7:15] I do not understand my own actions. For I do not do what I want, but I do the very thing I hate. [16] Now if I do what I do not want, I agree that the law is good. [17] But in fact it is no longer I that do it, but sin that dwells within me. [18] For I know that nothing good dwells within me, that is, in my flesh. I can will what is right, but I cannot do it. [19] For I do not do the good I want, but the evil I do not want is what I do. [20] Now if I do what I do not want, it is no longer I that do it, but sin that dwells within me.

[21] So I find it to be a law that when I want to do what is good, evil lies close at hand. [22] For I delight in the law of God in my inmost self, [23] but I see in my members another law at war with the law of my mind, making me captive to the law of sin that dwells in my members. [24] Wretched man that I am! Who will rescue me from this body of death?

For Paul, and other anguished souls like him, such as Augustine of Hippo, rescue from the human predicament created by the troubled voice of conscience came from the Saviour Christ who did for them what they could not do for themselves. It is this heightening and tightening of the theological claim that makes a non-dogmatic reading of the New Testament difficult: difficult, but not, as we will see, impossible. If the summons of God to action against tyranny and oppression is the second theme of Exodus, then the third theme, the frightened human response to his challenge, is almost as powerful: "'I will send you to Pharaoh to bring my people, the Israelites, out of Egypt." [11] But Moses said to God, "Who am I that I should go to Pharaoh, and bring the Israelites out of Egypt?'" Moses is a reluctant hero, one of a long line of men in flight from their own demons who are called to do great things, and precipitate terrifying violence in doing them. In folk tales documented in many traditions of the ancient Near East, the hero who is destined to deliver an oppressed people from bondage is always threatened in his infancy by an evil ruler from whom he is saved by being hidden and subsequently rescued.[22] His adult character is marked by a hair-trigger temper, and an intense feeling of personal inadequacy; compassion for the suffering, and a burning sense of justice. The elements are all there in the Moses story, which becomes a template that will be used over and over again in the future. Flawed and uncertain, we can hear his growling reply to the call of destiny echoing down the ages, up to the Hollywood Westerns of our own day, particularly in Clint Eastwood's *Unforgiven*. When a cowboy cuts up the face of a prostitute and a bounty is placed on his head, Will Munny, played by Eastwood, sets out with his old partner, played by Morgan Freeman, to avenge the woman. The Egypt of the movie is the town of Big Whiskey, under the Pharaonic control of Sheriff Daggett, played by Gene Hackman. The film ends with its own bleak version of a demonic exodus, as Munny shoots up the town during a thunderstorm.

The exodus theme plays itself out in real life as well as in fiction. Its most poignant replay in recent history is the story of Martin Luther King's battle for civil rights in the USA. King, a classic Moses figure and master of exodus rhetoric, used the great biblical tropes in his courageous stand against the prejudices that held his own people in bondage. Tragically, and again like Moses, he was not himself to see the promised land of freedom and equality for his own people. He was assassinated at the Lorraine Motel in Memphis on 4 April 1968. The day before his murder he had delivered a speech which concluded with these prophetic words: 'Well, I don't know what will happen now; we've got some difficult days ahead. But it doesn't matter with me now, because I've been to the mountaintop. And I don't mind. Like anybody, I would like a long life – longevity has its place. But I'm not concerned about that now. I just want to do God's will. He's allowed me to go up to the mountain. And I've looked over, and I've seen the promised land. I may not get there with you. But I want you to know tonight, that we, as a people, will get to the promised land. And so I'm happy tonight; I'm not worried about anything; I'm not fearing any man. Mine eyes have seen the glory of the coming of the Lord.'

The mountaintop reference, so poignantly used by King, comes from the last chapter of the Book of Deuteronomy. Moses climbs Mount Pisgah, a peak in Transjordan east of Jericho, and God shows him the promised land in Deuteronomy:

> [34:4] 'This is the land of which I swore to Abraham, to Isaac, and to Jacob, saying, "I will give it to your descendants"; I have let you see it with your eyes, but you shall not cross over there.' [5] Then Moses, the servant of the Lord, died there in the land of Moab, at the Lord's command.

Which brings us to the fourth and most beautiful and tragic of the exodus themes, the longing for the permanent good place, the promised land. Like Moses, Martin Luther King was never to enter the promised land, but those who did soon realized that achieving the object of their longing never did fulfil their desire. The history of the Israelites, once they established themselves in Canaan, the fabled land of milk and honey, was a tale of decadence and unfaithfulness: the richness of the land given to them by God became the very thing that lured them from God. One strand in the biblical tradition would look back with longing to the innocent years in the wilderness before the Israelites were suffocated by the pleasures of Palestine. It was this searing disappointment with human affairs that sowed the seeds of the eschatological longing that would later flower in biblical apocalyptic: surely there would come a day when God would again erupt into human history and, this time, the promise would be delivered.

Before leaving the Israelites, either trudging in the wilderness or settling in the promised land, there is a final note we should listen to: the tragic vocation of the Jews in history. Israeli novelist David Grossman says: 'Exodus, the grand story of the childhood of the Jewish people, sketches the primordial face of that people as it is being formed and, as we now know, describes what will be its fate throughout thousands of years of history.'[23] No wonder the Hebrew Bible tells us the Israelites murmured against Moses and his elusive, invisible, unspeakable, demanding God. Who wouldn't?

> O God of Mercy
> For the time being
> Choose another people.
> We are tired of death, tired of corpses,
> We have no more prayers.
> For the time being
> Choose another people.[24]

3

CONNECTING

Deuteronomy [24:17–22; 25:1–4]
You shall not deprive a resident alien or an orphan of justice; you shall not take a widow's garment in pledge. [18] Remember that you were a slave in Egypt and the Lord your God redeemed you from there; therefore I command you to do this.

[19] When you reap your harvest in your field and forget a sheaf in the field, you shall not go back to get it; it shall be left for the alien, the orphan, and the widow, so that the Lord your God may bless you in all your undertakings. [20] When you beat your olive trees, do not strip what is left; it shall be for the alien, the orphan, and the widow.

[21] When you gather the grapes of your vineyard, do not glean what is left; it shall be for the alien, the orphan, and the widow. [22] Remember that you were a slave in the land of Egypt; therefore I am commanding you to do this.

[25:1] Suppose two persons have a dispute and enter into litigation, and the judges decide between them, declaring one to be in the right and the other to be in the wrong. [2] If the one in the wrong deserves to be flogged, the judge shall make that person lie down and be beaten in his presence with the number of lashes proportionate to the offence. [3] Forty lashes may be given but not more; if more lashes than these are given, your neighbour will be degraded in your sight. [4] You shall not muzzle an ox while it is treading out the grain.

In his novel *Howard's End* E. M. Forster, with sympathy as well as irony, explored the social and sexual hypocrisy of Edwardian England, represented by the residents of the country house in Hertfordshire from which the book got its title. As an epigraph to the novel, Forster famously coined the phrase: *Only Connect*. The theme of the book is the way most of his characters refuse to do this, and fail to connect their own vices, and the difficulties in which their vices land them, with their impact on others. In particular, Forster turns a moral searchlight on the hypocrisy of Henry Wilcox for refusing to help the needy Leonard Bast, because he is afraid it might reveal that in the past he had had an affair with his wife. This plea to connect our own failures sympathetically to the predicaments of others was not invented by Forster: it is a dominant theme in both the Hebrew Bible and the New Testament. Its bluntest expression is probably the story of the seduction of Bathsheba by King David in II Samuel.

> [11:1] In the spring of the year, the time when kings go out to battle, David sent Joab with his officers and all Israel with him; they ravaged the Ammonites, and besieged Rabbah. But David remained at Jerusalem.
> [2] It happened, late one afternoon, when David rose from his couch and was walking about on the roof of the king's house, that he saw from the roof a woman bathing; the woman was very beautiful. [3] David sent someone to inquire about the woman. It was reported, 'This is Bathsheba daughter of Eliam, the wife of Uriah the Hittite.' [4] So David sent messengers to get her, and she came to him, and he lay with her.

Weeks later Bathsheba tells David she is pregnant. Alarmed, he sends for her husband, hoping he will sleep with his wife and assume the child is his. Uriah refuses the opportunity of sexual pleasure while his brothers are still in danger on the battlefield, so David has him placed on the front line where he is killed. He then adds Bathsheba to his stable of wives. Cut to the next scene: Nathan the prophet visits the king and tells him about two men, one rich, the other poor; and how the rich man, with hundreds of sheep to his name, has stolen the single ewe lamb, the family pet, of the poor man. Outraged, David demands to know the offender's name so that he can have him punished and the poor man recompensed: 'Thou art the man,' says Nathan. Whatever else he is, David is no hypocrite: he immediately gets the connection, and repents. This summons to what we might call the ethic of solidarity in failure is also a strong theme in the teaching of Jesus. One of his parables is about a man who fails to connect: forgiven a colossal debt by his master, he then goes on to throw a poor man into prison over a tiny sum.[25]

The denunciation of blatant moral hypocrisy may be an open and obvious target for biblical ethics; what is more revolutionary is that the Bible also commands a type of solidarity that requires a deeper imaginative sympathy from people: it calls on them to connect their good fortune to the misfortunes of others. Its most powerful and beautiful expression is found in the chapter's opening extract from Deuteronomy, the fifth book of the Hebrew Bible. Deuteronomy is the Greek translation of an ancient Hebrew name for the book, meaning second law or repetition of the law, because it is crafted as a recapitulation of the law contained in the previous three books of the Pentateuch.[26] Deuteronomy is one of the most sustained and brilliant pieces of moral rhetoric in world literature. Although we are meant to imagine Moses delivering it as a series of valedictory sermons to the tribes gathered in Transjordan before they descended upon the promised land, its actual provenance

and audience are much later. Whatever its exact origins, the
Hebrew Bible tells us it was 'rediscovered' during the reign
of King Josiah in 640 BCE[27] and became the main instrument
in a reformation of morals in the restored kingdom of Judah.
Not the least of the virtues of this humanitarian classic is the
delicacy and tact it expects of the well-off when they try to
help the needy.

> [24:19] When you reap your harvest in your field and forget a sheaf
> in the field, you shall not go back to get it; it shall be left for the
> alien, the orphan, and the widow, so that the Lord your God may bless
> you in all your undertakings. [20] When you beat your olive trees, do
> not strip what is left; it shall be for the alien, the orphan, and the
> widow.
> [21] When you gather the grapes of your vineyard, do not glean
> what is left; it shall be for the alien, the orphan, and the widow. [22]
> Remember that you were a slave in the land of Egypt; therefore I am
> commanding you to do this.

In these verses the practical sympathy the listeners are to
strive for is not achieved by connecting their secret weaknesses
with the public misdemeanours of others, but by contrasting
their present liberty and good fortune with their previous
servitude. When reminded of a flaw in our own character
which we have condemned in others, most of us will have the
grace to blush with shame and own up or learn to keep silent
on the subject. Personal moral failure is the best teacher of
sympathy for the mistakes of others, and life brings us many
opportunities to acquire such magnanimity. For some reason
economic sympathy is harder to promote and more difficult to
sustain, maybe because worldly success often has a hardening
effect on the character. The Hebrew Bible and the New
Testament are at one in their condemnation of moral
hypocrisy; but they are even stronger in their agreement on

the coarsening effect of wealth on humanity. It is the emergence of this passionate ethical imperative that brings us to the next stage in biblical thinking about God.

Today we take the link between religion and social ethics absolutely for granted, forgetting that it was a revolutionary claim at the time, a leap in moral evolution that associated God, the fount of all power, with the ethic of human solidarity that called on the strong to care for the weak. The universal existence among religions of the practice of sacrifice, not excluding human sacrifice, suggests that the original human response to the gods was fear of their arbitrary and unpredictable power. The sacrifice system, though it was spiritualized later, was essentially a way of keeping the gods sweet, though it probably also had elements of a protection racket in it: the gods' clients would expect some return for their offerings. In its later development it provided a way of giving thanks for benefits received, as well as an opportunity for expiating moral and ritual offences. That accounts for the final elaboration of the sacrifice system among the Hebrews, which is laid out in careful detail in the early chapters of the priestly handbook called Leviticus, the third book of the Pentateuch. So far, so predictable.

What happened next was the appearance in history of what scholars label 'ethical monotheism', the idea that God was righteous as well as powerful. The discovery of the ethical dimension in God coincided with a remarkable evolution in human attitudes that occurred in a number of different places around the eighth century BCE. One of its most potent expressions was found among the heirs of the Hebrew slaves who escaped from Egypt and were now settled in their promised land of plenty. There arose among them a group of remarkable men who inveighed against the widening gulf between rich and poor in Israel. At the heart of their challenge to the prosperous Israelites who flocked to the temple to offer their gifts and sacrifices to God was the shocking claim that God did not want their worship; what he wanted was social justice and care for the poor. The rawest version of the message came from an angry crofter called Amos:

> [5:21] I hate, I despise your festivals,
>   and I take no delight in your solemn assemblies.
> [22] Even though you offer me your burnt offerings and grain offerings,
>   I will not accept them;
> and the peace offerings of your fatted beasts
>   I will not look upon.
> [23] Take away from me the noise of your songs;
>   I will not listen to the melody of your harps.
> [24] But let justice roll down like waters,
>   and righteousness like an ever-flowing stream.

God, it turned out, was not a vain despot with a depthless appetite for human flattery, but a moral being with a raging anger against inequality. He was indifferent to the rites and ceremonies that normally characterized the courts of the gods: what he wanted was affirmative action to correct the gross imbalance between rich and poor that was becoming such a feature of developing societies. Maybe because he was a realist about human nature, he called for radical amelioration rather than absolute revolution, but there is no doubt that the Bible places God solidly on the redistributionist rather than on the monetarist side of politics. Though he probably wasn't a Marxist, God was certainly a socialist who wanted more mutuality and less competition in society.

It was and remains a controversial stance. There have always been those who thought that an ethic that prompted the wealthy to share their good fortune with the poor was a mistake, because they believe that those who learn to depend upon others for support lose the will to struggle against adversity that is essential to survival in an implacable world. Implicit in the debate are two opposing attitudes towards the brute fact of the universe. The unsentimental view sees the universe as an overwhelming explosion of energy, thrusting through time and space, that is pitilessly indifferent to the trillions of casualties it leaves in its wake. In such a universe only those strong enough to pit themselves against the heedless rush of chaos can flourish: though only for a time, because the universe defeats everyone in the end. To feel pity for life's losers, and thrust help upon them, is ultimately unloving and counter-adaptive, because it weakens rather than strengthens them for the battle. Nietzsche certainly thought so. Personally a compassionate man, he thought that behind the emergence of the ethic of pity lay the resentment the weak inevitably feel for the strong: 'The slave revolt in morality begins when *ressentiment* itself becomes creative and gives birth to values: the *ressentiment* of natures that are denied the true reaction, that of deeds, and compensate themselves with an imaginary revenge. While every noble morality develops from a triumphant affirmation of itself, slave morality from the outset says "no" to what is "outside", what is "different", what is "not itself"; and *this* "no" is its creative deed. This inversion of the value-positing eye – this *need* to direct one's view outward instead of back to oneself – is of the essence of *ressentiment*: in order to exist, slave morality always first needs a hostile external world; it needs, physiologically speaking, external stimuli in order to act at all – its action is fundamentally reaction.'[28]

There are subtleties in that famous passage. Nietzsche is interested in the origin of values, the genealogy of morals.

The fact that a value had a lowly or even an unworthy origin no more undermines it than an oak tree is diminished by the knowledge that it started as an acorn. Wherever it came from, a value is now something we prize because of the contribution it makes to human good. Amos, and the Deuteronomist who followed him, believed that the ethic of human solidarity came from God, the fount of justice. Nietzsche believed that it came not from on high, but from below, from the revolt of slaves against their oppressors. But does it matter where it came from, as long as we are glad it came from somewhere? What Nietzsche really scorned was the refusal to acknowledge the lowly, maybe even the resentful, origin of what we now claim to be our highest values. He wanted to show us that, if we go back far enough, we will discover that even our highest ideals have a dark side. But once a useful value has been created does it matter where it came from? I don't think so; nor does Richard Rorty, the philosopher who is closest to the kind of practical reading of the Bible I am suggesting. He is less interested in the originating authority we establish for values than in the usefulness of the values themselves.

'Philosophers who see morals as resting on metaphysics, press such notions too hard when they ask questions like, "But *is* there a God?" or, "Do human beings really *have* these rights?" Such questions presuppose that moral progress is at least in part a matter of increasing moral knowledge, knowledge about something independent of our social practices; something like the will of God or the nature of humanity. This metaphysical suggestion is vulnerable to Nietzschean suggestions that both God and human rights are superstitions – contrivances put forward by the weak to protect themselves against the strong. Whereas metaphysicians reply to

Nietzsche by asserting that there is a "rational basis" for belief in God or in human rights, pragmatists reply by saying that there is nothing wrong with contrivances. The pragmatist can cheerfully agree with Nietzsche that the idea of human brotherhood would only occur to the weak – to the people being shoved around by the brave, strong, happy warriors whom Nietzsche idolizes. But for pragmatists this fact no more counts against the idea of human rights than Socrates' ugliness counts against his account of the nature of love, or Freud's little private neuroses count against *his* account of love, or Newton's theologico-astrological motivations count against his mechanics. Once you drop the distinction between reason and passion, you no longer discriminate against a good idea because of its origins. You classify ideas according to their relative utility rather than by their sources.'[29]

Rorty's bracing summons to drop the debate about the precise authority for morality and get on with making the world a better place sounds to me a bit like the unknowable, invisible, untouchable God who called upon Moses, Amos and the author of Deuteronomy to forget liturgy and metaphysics and get on with making the world more just. It may require a high level of moral imagination for the prosperous and successful to sympathize with the poor, especially if they think of them as undeserving, but the Bible undoubtedly thinks they ought to, because it knows that radically unequal societies are less happy, less healthy and much more violent and turbulent, than those that care for their weaker members. That is probably why the Bible calls us to the practice of imaginative sympathy for the poor: to leave the forgotten sheaf in the field, and not to strip the olive tree or the grape vine bare. However we account for it, the emergence of practical sympathy for others from the empty indifference of the universe is almost as miraculous an event as the eruption of the universe itself out of that other abyss of emptiness. And even Nietzsche threw his arms round the neck of a defence-less beaten horse, and wept. Only connect.

4

EXILE

Isaiah [40:1] Comfort, O comfort my people,
   says your God.
[2] Speak tenderly to Jerusalem,
   and cry to her
that she has served her term,
   that her penalty is paid,
that she has received from the Lord's hand
   double for all her sins.

[3] A voice cries out:
'In the wilderness prepare the way of the Lord,
   make straight in the desert a highway for our God.
[4] Every valley shall be lifted up,
   and every mountain and hill be made low;
the uneven ground shall become level,
   and the rough places a plain.
[5] Then the glory of the Lord shall be revealed,
   and all people shall see it together,
   for the mouth of the Lord has spoken.'
[9] Get you up to a high mountain,
   O Zion, herald of good tidings;
lift up your voice with strength,
   O Jerusalem, herald of good tidings,
   lift it up, do not fear;

say to the cities of Judah,
  'Here is your God!'
[10] See, the Lord God comes with might,
  and his arm rules for him;
his reward is with him,
  and his recompense before him.
[11] He will feed his flock like a shepherd;
  he will gather the lambs in his arms,
and carry them in his bosom,
  and gently lead the mother sheep.

A few years ago I went to Geneva to make a television programme about the great Scottish Reformer John Knox, who
had spent some of his happiest years in that city as a friend and
disciple of John Calvin, the father of the most radical version
of Protestantism in sixteenth-century Europe. We filmed in
the great medieval cathedral, now a Protestant Church, which
was once bright with the colour of imagery and heavy with
the smoke of incense. Calvin stripped it bare, and bare it
remains, a sort of desert in stone, from which everything has
been removed that might interrupt the soul's pure encounter
with God. As someone who prefers religions that let the transcendent shine through the windows of the senses, its fierce
and uncompromising emptiness made me shiver, though I
was impressed by its audacity.

The story of the cathedral in Geneva encapsulates an
ancient tension within Christianity, which can be traced right
back to the Hebrew settlement in the promised land. At the
heart of the tension lies the ambiguity of the response of religion to human culture. The most common definition of
culture is any widespread behaviour that is transmitted by
learning rather than acquired by inheritance. On the basis of
that definition, culture is the most distinctly human thing

about us. We have many things in common with the other animals with whom we share the planet, including an inherited drive to propagate ourselves, but the thing that is most distinctive about us is what we learn from the legacy of humanity's creative response to the world. As well as feeding, sheltering and propagating ourselves, we have built cities, composed symphonies, painted pictures, written books, invented science and philosophy, founded complex civilizations and developed religions that sought to express the mystery of humanity's struggle to understand its own existence and the universe in which it is set. Part of that struggle is the ambivalence of some religions to the more developed forms of human culture. Is human culture a rival or an ally of God? Does the lure and fascination of art, science and philosophy draw the soul away from its search for God, or is human culture itself best interpreted as having been inspired by the Creator himself? Though there are mediating positions between them, there have been two extreme responses to those questions, one seeing human culture as a manifestation of the glory of God, the other seeing it as a dangerous rival to God. It was the former impulse that lavished colour and ornamentation upon the cathedral in Geneva, in order to proclaim the beauty of a God who made himself immanent in the richness of human creativity; but it was the latter impulse that stripped it bare again, in order to proclaim the forbidding truth that God was utterly transcendent above human culture and must be approached nakedly and in fear and trembling. This tension lies behind the not-unfounded suspicion that cities, with all their temptations and distractions, are more likely to lure souls away from pure religion than the innocence of wild places. A steady theme in the Hebrew scriptures is the coming of a prophet from the purity of the wilderness into a teeming and faithless city to call it to repent and return to God. It is there in the Christian scriptures as well, notably in the opening verses of Mark's Gospel:

[1] The beginning of the good news of Jesus Christ, the Son of God. [2] As it is written in the prophet Isaiah, 'See, I am sending my messenger ahead of you, who will prepare your way; [3] the voice of one crying out in the wilderness: "Prepare the way of the Lord, make his paths straight"', [4] John the baptizer appeared in the wilderness, proclaiming a baptism of repentance for the forgiveness of sins. [5] And people from the whole Judean countryside and all the people of Jerusalem were going out to him, and were baptized by him in the river Jordan, confessing their sins.

A foreshadowing of the danger human culture would pose for religion can be traced back to the long struggle for the soul of Israel that followed the settlement in Canaan. The metaphor that best captures the tension is the idea of Israel as God's bride, faithful and loving to him during the honeymoon years they spent together in the wilderness, but seduced away from him by the blandishments of the gods of the more developed communities they encountered in Canaan. The anger of God at the chosen people's adultery with other gods was proclaimed through the phenomenon of prophecy; prophecy not as prediction or soothsaying, but as an outpouring of the raw grief of a jealous God at the unfaithfulness of his people, and the disaster it portended. Understood historically, therefore, prophecy is essentially a theological interpretation of the politics of the settlement in Canaan and the struggle to build a nation that followed. What we get is history refracted through the lens of religion. To get the picture we have to take a quick look at the turbulent history of the Hebrew monarchy.

After the struggles of the early years in Canaan, recorded in Joshua and Judges, the monarchy was finally solidified under David – as potent a figure in Hebrew history as Moses. The First and Second Books of Samuel describe David's fight to establish himself as undisputed king. The First and Second Books of Kings take up the story at the consolidation of the monarchy around 970 BCE under Solomon, the son of David and Bathsheba.[30] But the monarchy was not to endure as a single entity: after Solomon's death the land was divided into two kingdoms, Israel in the north, Judah in the south. According to the prophetic understanding of history, the story was never about the rivalrous politics of small chieftaincies trying to hold their own against larger predatory neighbours; it was always about religious unfaithfulness, resulting in loss of independence and ultimate exile. Israel, the northern kingdom, was the first to go. It fell to the Assyrian Empire somewhere round 721 BCE.[31] Judah, the southern kingdom, survived by paying tribute to the Assyrians, but it became a client state with a precarious existence. It finally collapsed in 597 BCE, and its leaders were led into exile. The Book of Isaiah provides a prophetic backdrop to the three acts of the unfolding saga in the southern kingdom: warnings about the consequences of Judah's unfaithfulness; the inevitable downfall of Jerusalem and the exile that followed; and the hope of a return to the land from which they had been banished.

Isaiah is not one book, covering one period, but at least two and probably three books, covering two hundred years of history. It has been rather unimaginatively described by scholars as First Isaiah, chapters 1–39; Second Isaiah (or Second and Third Isaiah), chapters 40–66. The first part of the book covers the work of the prophet Isaiah in Judah and Jerusalem in the eighth century BCE, during the critical period when the northern kingdom was annexed to the Assyrian Empire.[32] To borrow a term from twentieth-century British politics, Isaiah was a trenchant critic of the policies and practices of New Israel because it had forsaken the traditional values established by Moses as set forth in the great sermons of Deuteronomy. Isaiah was defiantly Old Israel, firmly set in the social justice tradition of Amos, Hosea and Micah, who were his direct contemporaries.

[5:1] Let me sing for my beloved
   my love-song concerning his vineyard:
My beloved had a vineyard
   on a very fertile hill.
[2] He dug it and cleared it of stones,
   and planted it with choice vines;
he built a watchtower in the midst of it,
   and hewed out a wine vat in it;
he expected it to yield grapes,
   but it yielded wild grapes.

[3] And now, inhabitants of Jerusalem
   and people of Judah,
judge between me
   and my vineyard.
[4] What more was there to do for my vineyard
   that I have not done in it?
When I expected it to yield grapes,
   why did it yield wild grapes?

[5] And now I will tell you
   what I will do to my vineyard.
I will remove its hedge,
   and it shall be devoured;
I will break down its wall,
   and it shall be trampled down.

[13] Therefore my people go into exile without knowledge;
their nobles are dying of hunger,
  and their multitude is parched with thirst.
[24] Therefore, as the tongue of fire devours the stubble,
  and as dry grass sinks down in the flame,
so their root will become rotten,
  and their blossom go up like dust;
for they have rejected the instruction of the Lord of hosts,
  and have despised the word of the Holy One of Israel.

The end came for Jerusalem in 597 BCE and Judah's leaders were led into exile in Babylon. But it was this very exile that supplied the occasion for a more consoling type of prophecy in which the eschatology of doom was to be replaced by an eschatology of hope. When we fast forward to 539 BCE the geopolitical situation has taken another one of its unplanned twists. The Assyrian Empire is about to be conquered by Cyrus, King of Persia. Just before the fall of Babylon to the advancing armies of the Persian ruler, we find the second prophetic voice contained in this book proclaiming a message of encouragement to God's chastened people:

[40:1] Comfort, O comfort my people,
  says your God.
[2] Speak tenderly to Jerusalem,
  and cry to her
that she has served her term,
  that her penalty is paid,
that she has received from the Lord's hand
  double for all her sins.

It is to be through the agency of his servant, Cyrus, that God will restore Judah to its appointed place: indeed, even as the prophet speaks, a highway is being prepared for them, along which they will travel to the land of their heart's desire. The first of the exiles to return went back in 538 BCE.

> [3] A voice cries out:
>   In the wilderness prepare the way of the Lord,
>   make straight in the desert a highway for our God.
> [9] Get you up to a high mountain,
>   O Zion, herald of good tidings;
> lift up your voice with strength,
>   O Jerusalem, herald of good tidings,
>   lift it up, do not fear;
> say to the cities of Judah,
>   'Here is your God!'

Consoling as this restoration was, it was the experience of exile that would leave its enduring mark on the character of Hebrew religion. It was the final loss of geographical and national identity that began to establish the extraordinary character of Judaism as a religious and cultural phenomenon that has endured to our own day, and it brings us back to the conflict about human culture with which we began this chapter. The danger of religions that, however subtly, locate God within human culture and identify his presence with places and forms and ceremonies is that they can easily become substitutes for God rather than windows through which his transcendence can be mediated. This was the greatest fear of the prophetic tradition in Hebrew religion, idolatry: the worship of the created instead of the creator. To put it another way, rather than looking *through* the human construct that is meant to express something of the mystery of God, the disciple starts looking *at* it as though it were itself God. The great paradox of the Jewish experience was that it was Jerusalem that became God's greatest rival. The Jews had fallen so passionately in love with their promised land and its holy city, and had become so rooted in it, that they were in danger of substituting it for the invisible, inaudible God who had led them out of Egypt and who would brook no rivals in their affections. Their mistake was that when they lost Jerusalem they thought they had lost God as well:

Psalm [137:1] By the rivers of Babylon –
    there we sat down and there we wept
    when we remembered Zion.
[2] On the willows there
    we hung up our harps.
[3] For there our captors
    asked us for songs,
and our tormentors asked for mirth, saying,
    'Sing us one of the songs of Zion!'

[4] How could we sing the Lord's song
    in a foreign land?
[5] If I forget you, O Jerusalem,
    let my right hand wither!
[6] Let my tongue cling to the roof of my mouth,
    if I do not remember you,
if I do not set Jerusalem
    above my highest joy.

The gift had become more important to them than the giver. It was the fear that this might happen that had been the deepest horror of Hebrew religion: the worship of things crafted by human hands or human minds as a substitute for the inaudible, invisible mystery of God. It was this understandable human weakness for the tangible that had lured Aaron, Moses' assistant, to create for the Israelites a golden calf, something they could see and touch and bow before.[33] This was the reason Hebrew religion preferred even language about God to be indirect. It was the reason it banned the making of images of God. To this kind of hypersensitive monotheism even atheism was better than idolatry. It was better to empty the world of God entirely than to identify any human construct as God and call divine that which is only another flawed human work. To the spiritual genius of Hebrew religion this was and remains the greatest danger to humanity. It is an absolute refusal to conform to the chronic human need to bow before idols, whether physical, political, religious or conceptual.

It was a prescient anxiety that foresaw the glut of emotional idolatry that would characterize human history. It was as though God himself had listened to the oracles of the prophets he had sent to warn his people against the snares and temptations of the world. It was as though he recognized that his gift to them of a place on earth had begun to draw their hearts away from him. They had become entangled in the politics of power; they had been seduced by the very milk and honey he had given them as a reward for their long years of slavery. And it was as though it finally dawned on him that in order to keep his children faithful he would have to take from them everything he had given them, except the terrible gift of himself. Only that, and the scriptures that bore witness to it, would remain. Ultimately, they would even have to lose their place in the world. The precarious toehold they had once found on earth would be snatched from them. Finally, they would become a people without place, without a home in the world. It was this loss of place that was to purge Hebrew religion of the brutal certainties that were later to characterize its daughters, Christianity and Islam. Being religions rooted in the power of place, they would learn to fight to hold onto what was theirs and fight even harder to impose it on others.

This is all yet to come, of course. Here in Isaiah chapter 40 the loss of place is not yet utterly complete. There would be another return through the desert; and another temple would be built on the sacred soil of the promised land: but it is impossible not to see the terrible shadow of the future thrown back into the past, portending another destruction and another exile, this one lasting 2000 years. It would be this state of permanent exile that would forge the character of the Jews in a way poignantly expressed by one of their greatest thinkers, Hannah Arendt:

> . . . the Jewish people are a classic example of a worldless people maintaining themselves throughout thousands of years . . . this world-lessness which the Jewish people suffered in being dispersed, and which – as with all people who are pariahs – generated a special warmth among those who belonged, changed when the state of Israel was founded.

She believed that something important was lost with the establishment of the State of Israel, and what must now be presumed to be a final return from exile. After 2000 years in which the Jews never bore arms and never had either missionary empires or coloured slaves, a final solution was proposed to the mysterious problem of their enduring existence in a world that had always hated their religious intensity. Even in the gas ovens of Europe, fighting for breath, they continued to praise the invisible, inaudible mystery who had obsessed them for thousands of years. The theological enormity of it is best expressed in the most moving of the Holocaust novels, *The Last of the Just*, by André Schwarz-Bart: 'And praised be Auschwitz. So be it. Maindanek. The Eternal. Treblinka. And praised be Buchenwald. So be it. Mauthausen. The Eternal. Belzec. And praised be Sobibor. So be it. Chelmno. The Eternal. Ponary. And praised be Theresienstadt. So be it.

Bergen-Belsen. The Eternal. Janow. So be it. Neuengamme. The Eternal. Pustkow. And praised be . . .'[34]

But this time it was too much. They asked God to take back the divine glory of their genius, and let them, like other people, have a place they could call their own, even if they had to fight for it. So back they came at last to the old place: a final return from exile. But something was lost. Hannah Arendt goes on: 'Yes, one pays dearly for freedom. The specifically Jewish humanity signified by their worldlessness was something very beautiful . . . this standing outside all social connections, the complete open-mindedness and absence of prejudice that I experienced, especially with my mother, who also exercised it in relation to the whole Jewish community. Of course, a great deal was lost with the passing of all that. One pays for liberation.'[35]

She was right. The Jews finally found a place they could call their own. But they paid dearly for the privilege. They became like the rest of us: brutal and compromised. And God went into exile.

5

SUFFERING

Job 1:1–12; 19:1, 9–27

There was once a man in the land of Uz whose name was Job. That man was blameless and upright, one who feared God and turned away from evil. [2] There were born to him seven sons and three daughters. [3] He had seven thousand sheep, three thousand camels, five hundred yoke of oxen, five hundred donkeys, and very many servants; so that this man was the greatest of all the people of the east. [4] His sons used to go and hold feasts in one another's houses in turn; and they would send and invite their three sisters to eat and drink with them. [5] And when the feast days had run their course, Job would send and sanctify them, and he would rise early in the morning and offer burnt offerings according to the number of them all; for Job said, 'It may be that my children have sinned, and cursed God in their hearts.' This is what Job always did.

[6] One day the heavenly beings came to present themselves before the Lord, and Satan also came among them. [7] The Lord said to Satan, 'Where have you come from?' Satan answered the Lord, 'From going to and fro on the earth, and from walking up and down on it.' [8] The Lord said to Satan, 'Have you considered my servant Job? There is no one like him on the earth, a blameless and upright man who fears God and turns away from evil.' [9] Then Satan answered the Lord, 'Does Job fear God for nothing? [10] Have you not put a fence around him and his house and all that he has, on every side? You have blessed the work of his hands, and his possessions

have increased in the land. [11] But stretch out your hand now, and touch all that he has, and he will curse you to your face.' [12] The Lord said to Satan, 'Very well, all that he has is in your power; only do not stretch out your hand against him!' So Satan went out from the presence of the Lord.

[19:1] Then Job answered:

[9] 'He has stripped my glory from me,
   and taken the crown from my head.

[10] He breaks me down on every side, and I am gone,
   he has uprooted my hope like a tree.

[11] He has kindled his wrath against me,
   and counts me as his adversary.

[12] His troops come on together;
   they have thrown up siegeworks against me,
   and encamp around my tent.

[13] He has put my family far from me,
   and my acquaintances are wholly estranged from me.

[14] My relatives and my close friends have failed me;

[15] the guests in my house have forgotten me;
   my serving girls count me as a stranger;
   I have become an alien in their eyes.

[16] I call to my servant, but he gives me no answer;
   I must myself plead with him.

[17] My breath is repulsive to my wife;
   I am loathsome to my own family.

[18] Even young children despise me;
   when I rise, they talk against me.

[19] All my intimate friends abhor me,
   and those whom I loved have turned against me.

[20] My bones cling to my skin and to my flesh,
   and I have escaped by the skin of my teeth.

[21] Have pity on me, have pity on me, O you my friends,
   for the hand of God has touched me!

[22] Why do you, like God, pursue me,
   never satisfied with my flesh?

[23] 'O that my words were written down!
   O that they were inscribed in a book!

[24] O that with an iron pen and with lead
    they were engraved on a rock for ever!
[25] For I know that my Redeemer lives,
    and that at the last he will stand upon the earth;
[26] and after my skin has been thus destroyed,
    then in my flesh I shall see God,
[27] whom I shall see on my side,
    and my eyes shall behold, and not another.'

What is the theological difference between the terrorist atrocity of 11 September 2001 and the tsunami disaster of 26 December 2004? The answer is that the former is thought to be easier to justify theologically than the latter. The problem of suffering is a notoriously difficult issue for religions that believe in the existence of a good and loving creator who is transcendentally separated from his creation. Not all understandings of God share this difficulty. The philosopher Spinoza identified the universe as one substance, which he described as 'God or nature'. Everything that happens, therefore, happens, of necessity, in God, so there is no morally problematic separation between God and what goes on in the world. If, however, you posit a god who is transcendentally external to, yet is the creative cause of, nature; and if you further refine this idea of God to include the attributes of omnipotence, omniscience and moral perfection, as is the case in the developed Christian tradition; then you are faced with the difficulty of explaining the presence of suffering in a world created by such a being. The classic way of stating the dilemma for believers in such a God is that if he is omnipotent and omniscient then he can't be good, because omniscient omnipotence could surely have devised a better universe; but if he *is* good then he can't be omnipotent, because if he were he would surely alter reality to make it more benign. Theodicy – from the Greek words for 'God' and 'justice' – is the technical term used to characterize the department of theology that attempts to answer or justify the problem suffering poses for believers in God.

Some of the reactions to 9/11 and the Boxing Day tsunami offer us a glimpse into religious responses to this ancient dilemma. The most ancient view was that suffering was God's punishment for human wickedness. To be fair to the theory, it probably had an originally positive intention, and it was only later that negative deductions were made from it. The essential claim was that God rewarded his righteous and obedient children with prosperity. This may be an old teaching, but it is still very much with us: it is one of the fundamental convictions of American Christian Evangelicalism and is increasingly prevalent in the developing world. Sign up to the true God, it says, walk in his way, and he will cause you to prosper. Tithe your substance to God and his representatives on earth, and he will reward you. The most egregious version of the doctrine is found in Psalm 37:

[25] I have been young, and now am old,
    yet I have not seen the righteous forsaken
    or their children begging bread.
[26] They are ever giving liberally and lending,
    and their children become a blessing.
[27] Depart from evil, and do good;
    so you shall abide for ever.
[28] For the Lord loves justice;
    he will not forsake his faithful ones.
The righteous shall be kept safe for ever,
    but the children of the wicked shall be cut off.
[29] The righteous shall inherit the land, and live in it for ever.

This kind of metaphysical utilitarianism may strike us as

strange, but there is worse to come. The tipping point of the theory into deadly negativity happens in verse 28 of the psalm: not only does God actively reward the righteous with prosperity, but he actively punishes the wicked with adversity. The final step in the evolution of the idea is the claim that if you are suffering, if you are having a hard time, if you have lost everything, then God must be punishing you for your misdeeds, however secret and unknown they are to others. Anyone who has engaged in pastoral work with troubled people will recognize the enduring residue of this pernicious theory in the frequent cry: 'What have I done to deserve this? I tried to lead a good life; and then this happens.' And it operates at the group as well as the personal level. God not only punishes individuals for their own misdeeds – he punishes whole societies for the misdeeds of sinful individuals who happen to be in their midst. We heard this response to 9/11 from Jerry Falwell and Pat Robertson, the popes of American Christian Fundamentalism, whose initial reaction to the atrocity was to see it as God's wrath on the wickedness of liberal America. A similar accusation was heard from Muslim clerics in Indonesia after the tsunami on Boxing Day 2004: God was cleansing the land of the corrupting effects of Western tourism on their previously pure society. The important distinction between the two events, of course, is that human agency was responsible for the first one, while the second was what the insurance industry describes as an act of God; which brings me back to the question I asked at the beginning of this chapter. It is thought to be less theologically damaging for believers if their suffering is caused by human agency rather than the workings of nature. The classic justification here is that since God has given freedom of will to humans, they are themselves responsible for any suffering they cause; whereas earthquakes and tsunamis are a consequence of the natural structure of the earth God created, so final responsibility for any suffering they effect must lie with him. This seems to me to be a distinction without much of a difference: if an omniscient and omnipotent manufacturer engineers a line of free-thinking creatures that malfunction and hurt each other, surely he, not the machines he designed, must be held to be ultimately responsible? On the whole, the Bible is indifferent to this kind of philosophical agonizing, with one glorious exception: the Book of Job. Job does not attempt to solve the problem of suffering for believers, but he effectively demolishes the most persistent answer to the predicament, which is that it is God's punishment for sin.

The book as we have it is a constantly worked-over folk tale that may be 3000 years old, though in its present form it probably comes from an anonymous poet of the Exile writing in the sixth century BCE. Though Job never removes the difficulty suffering poses for believers, he utterly undermines the most stubborn component of the traditional response. The folk-tale elements of the story are at their clearest in the opening two chapters, where, at the prompting of Satan, God plans a test to prove whether Job's piety is sincere or just a prudent calculation to guarantee his continued prosperity. Even at this stage in the tale a subtle undermining of the official theory is going on: we know that Job is undoubtedly righteous, so his prosperity could be said to lend support to the traditional view; but we also know that, for no reason other than his own whimsical interest in the test, God is about to deprive Job of the official rewards of genuine virtue. Job is baffled by the tsunami of loss and sorrow that engulfs him; but rather than submit himself to the oppressive certainty of the official doctrine and grovel before the Almighty, he calls upon

God to justify his conduct. Job knows that whatever is happening to him can't be a theological quid pro quo or tit for tat, because there was no 'quo' to justify the 'quid'. The philosophical heart of the book is the elaborate series of encounters between Job and three old pals, all fervent exponents of the official theory. They have come, no doubt with some sympathy for their friend, to get him to fess up and admit he has been up to something, which can be the only possible explanation for his condition. Eliphaz the Temanite goes first, and they all say the same thing over and over again, with increasing irritation:

[4:1] Then Eliphaz the Temanite answered:
[2] 'If one ventures a word with you, will you be offended?
    But who can keep from speaking?
[3] See, you have instructed many;
    you have strengthened the weak hands.
[4] Your words have supported those who were stumbling,
    and you have made firm the feeble knees.
[5] But now it has come to you, and you are impatient;
    it touches you, and you are dismayed.
[7] 'Think now, who that was innocent ever perished?
    Or where were the upright cut off?
[8] As I have seen, those who plough iniquity
    and sow trouble reap the same.
[9] By the breath of God they perish,
    and by the blast of his anger they are consumed.'

It has to be admitted that the book has its *longueurs*. In spite of the grandeur of the language, one soon longs for an end to the tedious sermonizing of Eliphaz the Temanite, Bildad the Shuhite and Zophar the Naamathite, not to mention the insufferable Elihu the Buzite, who is tacked on at the end – tedious archetypes of religious self-righteousness, all of them. Like religious and political system-thinkers everywhere and at all times, Job's friends are unable to see anything with new eyes: everything has to adapt to the official view; awkward facts have to be altered to fit the only allowable explanatory paradigm. That is why it never occurs to them that the received theory might be wrong and Job right. Were they to go down that avenue of possibility everything in their mechanistic universe would become unsteady. Better to stick to the theory, even if you have to sacrifice your friend on its behalf, than thrust yourself into the painful uncertainty of a world in which you have to think your way through moral complexity. For such a mind, it is always expedient that one or one million die than that the paradigm perish.[36] Identifying this kind of slavish addiction to official theory seems to have been the intention of the subversive artist who crafted the final version of the text. Baffled and angry, Job sticks to his story. He becomes a whistle-blower, an ordinary man who suddenly finds the courage to challenge a brutal theory. He may previously have been an unthinking believer in the official doctrine of suffering, but he knows that in his case a mistake has been made; he does not deserve this, and he is not afraid to say so, even to God. If the evidence is never discovered that will vindicate him in this life, he trusts that after his death, his advocate, his friend in court, traditionally the next of kin of the accused – misleadingly translated 'redeemer' in our text – will speak up for him before God and vindicate his reputation:

[19:25] For I know that my Redeemer lives,
    and that at the last he will stand upon the earth;
[26] and after my skin has been thus destroyed,
    then in my flesh I shall see God,
[27] whom I shall see on my side,
    and my eyes shall behold, and not another.

But Job does not have to wait for death to get his vindication. God appears on the scene at the end of the book and gives him his moment in court:

> [38:1] Then the Lord answered Job out of the whirlwind:
> [2] 'Who is this that darkens counsel by words without knowledge?
> [3] Gird up your loins like a man,
>   I will question you, and you shall declare to me.
> [4] Where were you when I laid the foundation of the earth?
>   Tell me, if you have understanding.'

Whatever you make of God's performance here, it leaves the problem of suffering unresolved. George Bernard Shaw described this speech as a divine sneer; but one theologian has said that the central affirmation of the book is God's verdict that the impious Job is a better theologian than his pious friends.[37] I can see what he means, but I think it is closer to the truth to say that Job sets his face against theology and its 'irritable reaching after fact and reason', to quote John Keats.[38] Job belongs to the noble army of people down the ages who have challenged the oppressive power of official ideas, not excluding ideas about God. The Hebrew intellectual tradition has been a richer and braver contributor to this dissident tradition than the two faith cultures it spawned: Christianity and Islam. Judaism is one long argument, most of it with God, whereas Christianity and Islam have a strong addiction to orthodox thinking and the behavioural conformity it inculcates. My main complaint about their argument with God is that they let him get away with murder: just the way Job does.

> [42:1] Then Job answered the Lord:
> [2] 'I know that you can do all things,
>   and that no purpose of yours can be thwarted.

[3] "Who is this that hides counsel without knowledge?"
Therefore I have uttered what I did not understand,
  things too wonderful for me, which I did not know.
[4] "Hear, and I will speak;
  I will question you, and you declare to me."
[5] I had heard of you by the hearing of the ear,
  but now my eye sees you;
[6] therefore I despise myself,
  and repent in dust and ashes.'

A bit of me wishes that Job, instead of abasing himself, had listened to his wife at the beginning of the book, when she said to him: [2:9] 'Do you still persist in your integrity? Curse God, and die.' Had Job done so, he would have placed himself in a long and honourable tradition of moral protest against the idea that any God worthy of human respect could preside over such a pain-soaked planet as ours. But this is not what Job does. He does not curse God; instead, he curses theology and its explanatory certainties. Intriguingly, this is what God does as well. God does not denounce Job the dissident, Job the heretic. Instead, he denounces the official theologians who have tried to press Job onto the Procrustean bed of orthodox theory: [42:7]' . . . the Lord said to Eliphaz the Temanite: "My wrath is kindled against you and against your two friends; for you have not spoken of me what is right, as my servant Job has."'

It has to be admitted that if we are after answers to the problem of suffering, then reading the book of Job will prove to be a disappointment. There are two possible routes to the resolution of the problem suffering poses for believers in God. One is to abandon the belief: in Mrs Job's words, to curse God. In a godless universe suffering ceases to be a theological problem and becomes, instead, a grim and ugly fact. The other possible resolution is to find a satisfactory theological answer that vindicates God. Though the Book of Job goes down neither of these avenues, implicit within it there is another response to the problem. Those who follow this third approach find all theological justifications of suffering morally repugnant, but this does not lead them to abandon God. Instead, they respond to suffering practically by doing all they can to alleviate it. For the rest, they choose to remain silent in its presence.

6

MESSIAH

When this boy, Jesus, was five years old, he was playing at the ford of a rushing stream. He was collecting the flowing water into ponds and made the water instantly pure. He did this with a single command. He then made soft clay and shaped it into twelve sparrows. He did this on the Sabbath day, and many other boys were playing with him. But when a Jew saw what Jesus was doing while playing on the Sabbath day, he immediately went off and told Joseph, Jesus' father: 'See here, your boy is at the ford and has taken mud and fashioned twelve birds with it, and so has violated the Sabbath.' So Joseph went there, and as soon as he spotted him he shouted, 'Why are you doing what's not permitted on the Sabbath?' But Jesus simply clapped his hands and shouted to the sparrows: 'Be off, fly away, and remember me, you who are now alive.' And the sparrows took off and flew away noisily.[39]

As well as the four gospels, Matthew, Mark, Luke and John, which made it into the New Testament, there are a number of other texts about Jesus that did not receive the Church's official attestation. Some of them contain miracle stories that are more exotic than the comparatively restrained versions found in the official gospels. One of these documents, quoted above, is *The Infancy Gospel of Thomas*, which survives in various forms in a number of languages, including Syriac, Greek, Latin and Slavonic. Though it may date from around the middle of the second century CE, the earliest extant manuscript is in Syriac, dating from the sixth century CE.[40] It confines itself to incidents in the boyhood of Jesus, such as the one quoted above.

Let me suggest a possible way in to understanding the thinking behind this strange little story that can help us in our approach to the infancy narratives in the official gospels of Matthew and Luke. When I go to the cinema I often prefer the previews to the full-length features, because they usually give you the best bits, tasters of what is to come. Trailers give you information about the next presentation, and they whet your appetite for it, make you eager to see it. Ancient writers used a version of this technique when they wrote about the childhood of great figures. Following the custom of their trade, they previewed or foreshadowed important themes in the life they were about to describe. The story from *The Infancy Gospel of Thomas* is a good example of the craft; but it also demonstrates how easy it is for a modern reader to misread an old text. The student today is likely to focus on the miracle described in the passage, since the miraculous is an awkward category for us to deal with: but for the author the miracle was incidental to his real intention, which was to prefigure the attitude of Jesus to the Sabbath, something that would be a major theme in his later ministry. Though he never used philosophical abstractions in his teaching, behind much of what Jesus said and did lay an important distinction between instrumental and intrinsic goods, between things that are good for something else, and things that are good in themselves. The Sabbath is the most controversial illustration of the principle: it is obviously good to give people days off, down-time; but it is the principle of rest that is important, not the particular way we express it, nor the day in the week by which we mark it. In other words, it is an instrumental not an intrinsic good. The Sabbath can never be an absolute, and in practice the Jews did not actually believe it was: they knew it would be absurd to refuse to rescue someone who was drowning because it would involve activity forbidden on the Sabbath, since saving a life is more important than taking a nap. Nevertheless, there are always people in any culture who fail to make the fundamental moral distinction between process and purpose, and they have a tendency to convert means into ends. We'll discuss this issue in greater depth later in the book: the point of the little story about Jesus making birds out of clay and giving them life on the Sabbath is that it's a trailer that points ahead to what will be an important theme in the life of this child when he becomes an adult. In Luke we find another of these childhood narratives, and we should read it not as a page from Mary's journal of life with Jesus, but as another example of the way ancient writers practised their craft.

Luke [2:41] Now every year his parents went to Jerusalem for the festival of the Passover. [42] And when he was twelve years old, they went up as usual for the festival. [43] When the festival was ended and they started to return, the boy Jesus stayed behind in Jerusalem, but his parents did not know it. [44] Assuming that he was in the group of travellers, they went a day's journey. Then they started to look for him among their relatives and friends. [45] When they did not find him, they returned to Jerusalem to search for him. [46] After three days they found him in the temple, sitting among the teachers, listening to them and asking them questions. [47] And all who heard him were amazed at his understanding and his answers. [48] When his parents saw him they were astonished; and his mother said to him, 'Child, why have you treated us like this? Look, your

father and I have been searching for you in great anxiety.' [49] He
said to them, 'Why were you searching for me? Did you not know that
I must be in my Father's house?' [50] But they did not understand
what he said to them. [51] Then he went down with them and came
to Nazareth, and was obedient to them.

Before trying to uncover the theme this passage is previewing for us, we ought to take a second or two to reflect on
how awkwardly it sits in its present place. Luke has already
told us in the first chapter of his gospel that an angel had
appeared to Mary and told her that she would give birth to
one who would be 'great, and will be called the Son of the
Most High, and the Lord God will give to him the throne of
his ancestor David. He will reign over the house of Jacob for
ever, and of his kingdom there will be no end.'41 Yet here we
are, twelve years later, with Mary expressing amazement at
finding her son in the temple demonstrating his profound
knowledge of the law. The most telling sentence is verse fifty:
'. . . they did not understand what he said to them.' They did
not understood their son's precocity, yet the angel of the Lord
had briefed them quite specifically on his real status: so why
the surprise? It is obvious that these two passages are out of
sync, which is why some scholars believe that the story of the
boy Jesus in the Temple is a piece of independent tradition
that Luke has slotted into his text without bothering to amend
it to conform to his general editorial line. Scholars have developed an intriguing vocabulary to describe the different layers
of text they have to deal with when they excavate the documentary geology of the New Testament: they would call this
little slice of narrative about the child Jesus 'a floating *pericope*',
from the Greek for a 'little cut (or snip) of text'. What we
might describe as the theological point of this pericope, the

theme in the life of Jesus that is being foreshadowed, is the presence in him of a commitment to God so intense that it relativizes all other loyalties. Jesus will be no celebrant of family values or tribal allegiances. For him, nothing that is humanly created deserves absolute authority: only God is God. In this he will be radically at one with the prophetic tradition that feared the cruel power of idolatry above all other human tendencies.

When studying ancient stories about Jesus, a characteristic that is just as important as the previewing of important themes from his life is the inclusion of developed understandings of his nature and divine status that were actually evolved much later. This has been described as 'the backward development of New Testament Christology'. Christology is the department of Christian theology that deals with the status and significance of Jesus. Even within the synoptic gospels the gradation in the disciples' estimation of Jesus moves from the human to the almost-divine. In a famous passage at the end of Luke, for example, two disciples are walking disconsolately to the village of Emmaus after the death of Jesus when he appears to them and upbraids them for being so slow to understand his significance as the one who had come to fulfil the scripture.[42] This trajectory of interpretation continued to move well into the first few centuries of the Church's existence, but we can trace its early development in the gospels. The four gospels were probably written between 65 and 90 CE: Mark was almost certainly the earliest, and John the latest; with Matthew and Luke somewhere in the middle of that spread of time. When the gospels came to be written, however, the evangelists read their mature understanding of Jesus as the Son of God back into the narratives they created about him. So Mark traces the divine status of Jesus back to his baptism by John in the river Jordan – he was adopted by God at that moment, when the heavens opened and a divine voice pronounced him his beloved son;[43] Matthew and Luke trace his status as the divine son back to his miraculous conception;[44] and John, the last and most Christologically developed of the four, takes him back to a time before time in the eternal life of God, proclaiming that in Jesus the pre-existing Word of God had taken flesh.[45] Adapting the nineteenth-century philosopher Kierkegaard's observation that we all live life forward but understand it backward, we could say that though the disciples lived their encounter with Jesus forward, they read their completed understanding of his nature backward into the stories they later wrote about him. What we should expect to find in the nativity stories of Matthew and Luke, therefore, is not so much recorded history, as retrospective theology. And it is the fact that they are offering different theological interpretations of the status of Jesus that accounts for the inconsistencies in their approach to the history.

Matthew [2:1] In the time of King Herod, after Jesus was born in Bethlehem of Judea, wise men from the East came to Jerusalem, [2] asking, 'Where is the child who has been born king of the Jews? For we observed his star at its rising, and have come to pay him homage.' [3] When King Herod heard this, he was frightened, and all Jerusalem with him; [4] and calling together all the chief priests and scribes of the people, he inquired of them where the Messiah was to be born. [5] They told him, 'In Bethlehem of Judea; for so it has been written by the prophet:
[6] "And you, Bethlehem, in the land of Judah,
    are by no means least among the rulers of Judah;
    for from you shall come a ruler
    who is to shepherd my people Israel."'
[7] Then Herod secretly called for the wise men and learned from

them the exact time when the star had appeared. [8] Then he sent them to Bethlehem, saying, 'Go and search diligently for the child; and when you have found him, bring me word so that I may also go and pay him homage.' [9] When they had heard the king, they set out; and there, ahead of them, went the star that they had seen at its rising, until it stopped over the place where the child was. [10] When they saw that the star had stopped, they were overwhelmed with joy. [11] On entering the house, they saw the child with Mary his mother; and they knelt down and paid him homage. Then, opening their treasure chests, they offered him gifts of gold, frankincense, and myrrh. [12] And having been warned in a dream not to return to Herod, they left for their own country by another road.

[13] Now after they had left, an angel of the Lord appeared to Joseph in a dream and said, 'Get up, take the child and his mother, and flee to Egypt, and remain there until I tell you; for Herod is about to search for the child, to destroy him.' [14] Then Joseph got up, took the child and his mother by night, and went to Egypt, [15] and remained there until the death of Herod. This was to fulfil what had been spoken by the Lord through the prophet, 'Out of Egypt I have called my son.'

Luke [2:1] In those days a decree went out from Emperor Augustus that all the world should be registered. [2] This was the first registration and was taken while Quirinius was governor of Syria. [3] All went to their own towns to be registered. [4] Joseph also went from the town of Nazareth in Galilee to Judea, to the city of David called Bethlehem, because he was descended from the house and family of David. [5] He went to be registered with Mary, to whom he was engaged and who was expecting a child. [6] While they were there, the time came for her to deliver her child. [7] And she gave birth to her firstborn son and wrapped him in bands of cloth, and laid him in a manger, because there was no place for them in the inn.

[8] In that region there were shepherds living in the fields, keeping watch over their flock by night. [9] Then an angel of the Lord stood before them, and the glory of the Lord shone around them, and they were terrified. [10] But the angel said to them, 'Do not be afraid; for see – I am bringing you good news of great joy for all the people: [11] to you is born this day in the city of David a Saviour, who is the Messiah, the Lord. [12] This will be a sign for you: you will find

a child wrapped in bands of cloth and lying in a manger.' [13] And suddenly there was with the angel a multitude of the heavenly host, praising God and saying,
[14] 'Glory to God in the highest heaven,
   and on earth peace among those whom he favours!'

It is pointless to dwell on the inconsistencies between the accounts of the birth of Jesus offered by Matthew and Luke. The historical difficulty presented by the fact that Luke knows nothing of the flight into Egypt – which is such a feature of Matthew's narrative – or that Matthew knows nothing of a chorus of angels and a gang of shepherds – which is such a feature of Luke's narrative – disappears when we remember John Dominic Crossan's formula that the gospels present us not with history remembered, but with prophecy historicized. The nativity narratives in Matthew and Luke are theology not history; they offer us coded interpretations of the life of one who had fulfilled the ancient Jewish longing for an agent anointed by God – *mashiach* in Hebrew, *christos* in Greek – who would restore the kingdom of the Jews. Matthew may have been writing for Jewish Christians who were tempted to abandon the Jesus movement when it became increasingly difficult to sustain their double loyalty in the local synagogue. Their loyalties were strained, particularly during the painful years that succeeded the final destruction of the Temple in Jerusalem by the Romans in 70 CE, and scholars generally date the writing of Matthew after this, somewhere between 80 and 90 CE. Matthew tries to fortify their allegiance by showing that Jesus is the new Moses. When Moses was born, Pharaoh slaughtered all the male children of the Hebrews in Egypt, so Matthew gives his readers a parallel massacre by Herod of all the male children in the region of Bethlehem who were two years old and younger.

According to Robert Funk, this kind of slaughter was a reg-
ular feature of biographies of heroes and in tales of royal
succession the world over: a king kills or exiles successors to
protect his own position. He claims that, while Herod the
Great was capable of slaughtering babies – after all, he had his
own three sons put to death – the story of the massacre of the
innocents is undoubtedly a fiction.[46] I would prefer to call it
a theological construct, an attempt by Matthew to establish
Jesus as the completion or consummation of the great line of
the heroes of Israel, including, in particular, Moses and David.
Even the mysterious wise men contribute to the Moses par-
allelism, according to the distinguished New Testament
scholar Raymond Brown, because in Jewish legends of this
time the pharaoh received information from wise men.[47] And
just as Moses led the Israelites out of Egypt to the promised
land, so Jesus flees to and returns from Egypt to Israel. We
may find this kind of theologico-historical creativity naïvely
mendacious, but it was the way Matthew established the messianic pedigree of Jesus.

Luke's theological aim is even more ambitious than
Matthew's: if Matthew sets out to establish Jesus as the suc-
cessor of Moses and the fulfilment of the history of Israel,
Luke is placing him at the centre of a world narrative. For
Matthew, Jesus eclipses Moses; for Luke, however, Jesus
eclipses the supreme ruler Caesar Augustus, which is why he
provides a Roman setting for his birth, during a census
decreed by the Emperor, 'the first registration . . . taken
while Quirinius was governor of Syria'. Theologically this
claim may be apt; historically, it is just plain inaccurate.
There never was a census of the whole Roman Empire
under Augustus, though there were a number of local cen-
suses. The Judean census under Quirinius, the Governor of

Syria, took place in 6–7 CE, about ten years too late for the birth of Jesus, which is usually reckoned to have been somewhere around 4 BCE. We either have to conclude that Luke got his history badly wrong or, the option I prefer, that he was not that interested in historical fact other than as a vehicle for a theological claim. For him, this was the birth of a new kind of supreme ruler, a spiritual emperor whose territory would one day eclipse the might of Rome. This royal birth was announced not by imperial heralds, but by a multitude of the heavenly host, 'praising God and saying, "Glory to God in the highest heaven, and on earth peace among those whom he favours!"'

Modern readers may find this all a bit over the top; the uncanny thing is, whatever you make of the historiography of Matthew and Luke, the man they wrote about fulfilled their predictions to become the most famous figure in history.

There is something else in Luke's nativity narrative we ought to pay attention to. As well as establishing the royal spirituality of Jesus, he uses his narrative to preview a theme that will be important in the life he is about to describe: the identification of Jesus with the poor and outcast. Jesus is born in Bethlehem, the most insignificant of the cities of Judah. Shepherds, the gypsies or travelling people of his day, mistrusted and feared by the settled, are the first to hear of the birth. He is placed in a manger in the part of the house where the animals sleep, probably because they are staying with relatives who, though poor themselves, welcome them under their own roof. Luke clearly places Jesus at the bottom of the social pyramid. This is more than a romantic touch, with the king incognito, disguised as a peasant, but one day to step out of disguise and reveal his true royal identity. The low social status of Jesus was the true identity of the man of Nazareth. In what Nietzsche would have described as an act of transvaluation, Jesus was to identify God not with power, but with the victims of power. It is this reversal that is the key to understanding his character.

7

CHALLENGE

Matthew [5:1] When Jesus saw the crowds, he went up the mountain; and after he sat down, his disciples came to him. [2] Then he began to speak, and taught them, saying:

[3] 'Blessed are the poor in spirit, for theirs is the kingdom of heaven.

[4] 'Blessed are those who mourn, for they will be comforted.

[5] 'Blessed are the meek, for they will inherit the earth.

[6] 'Blessed are those who hunger and thirst for righteousness, for they will be filled.

[7] 'Blessed are the merciful, for they will receive mercy.

[8] 'Blessed are the pure in heart, for they will see God.

[9] 'Blessed are the peacemakers, for they will be called children of God.

[10] 'Blessed are those who are persecuted for righteousness' sake, for theirs is the kingdom of heaven.

[11] 'Blessed are you when people revile you and persecute you and utter all kinds of evil against you falsely on my account. [12] Rejoice and be glad, for your reward is great in heaven, for in the same way they persecuted the prophets who were before you.

[21] 'You have heard that it was said to those of ancient times, "You shall not murder"; and "whoever murders shall be liable to judgment." [22] But I say to you that if you are angry with a brother or sister, you will be liable to judgment; and if you insult a brother or sister, you will be liable to the council; and if you say, "You fool", you

will be liable to the hell of fire. [23] So when you are offering your gift at the altar, if you remember that your brother or sister has something against you, [24] leave your gift there before the altar and go; first be reconciled to your brother or sister, and then come and offer your gift. [25] Come to terms quickly with your accuser while you are on the way to court with him, or your accuser may hand you over to the judge, and the judge to the guard, and you will be thrown into prison. [26] Truly I tell you, you will never get out until you have paid the last penny.

[27] 'You have heard that it was said, "You shall not commit adultery." [28] But I say to you that everyone who looks at a woman with lust has already committed adultery with her in his heart. [29] If your right eye causes you to sin, tear it out and throw it away; it is better for you to lose one of your members than for your whole body to be thrown into hell. [30] And if your right hand causes you to sin, cut it off and throw it away; it is better for you to lose one of your members than for your whole body to go into hell.

[38] 'You have heard that it was said, "An eye for an eye and a tooth for a tooth." [39] But I say to you, Do not resist an evildoer. But if anyone strikes you on the right cheek, turn the other also; [40] and if anyone wants to sue you and take your coat, give your cloak as well; [41] and if anyone forces you to go one mile, go also the second mile. [42] Give to everyone who begs from you, and do not refuse anyone who wants to borrow from you.

[43] 'You have heard that it was said, "You shall love your neighbour and hate your enemy." [44] But I say to you, Love your enemies and pray for those who persecute you, [45] so that you may be children of your Father in heaven; for he makes his sun rise on the evil and on the good, and sends rain on the righteous and on the unrighteous. [46] For if you love those who love you, what reward do you have? Do not even the tax collectors do the same? [47] And if you greet only your brothers and sisters, what more are you doing than others? Do not even the Gentiles do the same? [48] Be perfect, therefore, as your heavenly Father is perfect.'

The block of text that is traditionally called the Sermon on the Mount is found in chapters five to seven of Matthew's gospel, and much debate has surged round its authenticity.

Did Jesus ever actually sit down on a hillside and preach a homily in the precise form recorded here? It is not impossible. It would only take about twenty minutes to deliver this material, a sermonette compared to the lengthy utterances many of his disciples have imposed upon long-suffering listeners down the centuries. Most scholars agree that it contains authentic sayings of Jesus, or strong echoes of authentic sayings of Jesus. However, two issues give scholars pause before deciding too confidently on which line to take. The first is something we have already noticed about Matthew's approach to his material. He is offering us not so much recorded history, as a highly sophisticated theological interpretation of the life of Jesus, the man who later became known as the Christ. We have already noticed how his infancy narrative was crafted to parallel the story of Moses; so it is likely that something similar is going on here. Just as Moses gave the law to the children of Israel on Mount Sinai,[48] so Jesus, the new Moses, delivered his teaching to his disciples, the new Israel, from a mountain.[49] The second fact that should give us pause is the knowledge we now have of the way the evangelists composed or redacted their narratives out of material that had a previous existence, either in extended form or in smaller cuts called pericopes. The most likely answer to the question about the setting of the sermon is that it is an intentional creation by Matthew, designed to parallel the Moses story. As far as the substance of the sermon is concerned, most of it was probably redacted by Matthew into its present form from other sources. That still leaves the big question unanswered: given that the setting of the sermon is a Matthean device; and that the substance of the sermon is a Matthean redaction; is the matter itself authentic, did Jesus actually say it somewhere? The answer to that depends on which scholars you listen to.

For instance, if you turn to the discussion of this material by the Jesus Seminar, using their famous colour code, you'll find a few verses in red, a few more in pink and grey, and quite a lot in black: which means that they think a lot of it was probably either said by Jesus, or something like it; while some of it undoubtedly was introduced from a later perspective.[50] A good example of an obviously inauthentic saying in the Sermon on the Mount, which is why I excluded it, is 5:17–19:

[17] 'Do not think that I have come to abolish the law or the prophets; I have come not to abolish but to fulfil. [18] For truly I tell you, until heaven and earth pass away, not one letter, not one stroke of a letter, will pass from the law until all is accomplished. [19] Therefore, whoever breaks one of the least of these commandments, and teaches others to do the same, will be called least in the kingdom of heaven; but whoever does them and teaches them will be called great in the kingdom of heaven.'

Since this clearly contradicts Jesus' relaxed attitude to the law, and since it is equally obvious that some of the more radical sayings of Jesus quoted in the sermon were intended to subvert or transvalue the received religious–legal tradition,[51] it would make sense to conclude that these verses are the work of a later author who was trying to soften the impact of Jesus' radicalism on the particular constituency he was targeting. If, as some scholars believe, Matthew's gospel was an appeal to Jewish Christians to stay within the Jesus movement and not revert to Judaism, then the passage's exaggerated reverence for the law, claiming as it does that not a single *iota* (the smallest letter of the Greek alphabet) – translated as 'one letter' in our passage – or *keraia* (the tiny stroke added to the end of a letter) – translated as 'one stroke of a letter' in our passage –

could ever be altered,[52] may be understandable, but it turns the whole message of Jesus on its head. It is reminiscent of how, during the British general election of 2005, Labour Party parliamentary candidates opposed to the Iraq War had to get round the fact that it was the leader of their own party who had led the country into it. Which brings us to the central challenge represented by this material.

The parts of the sermon that are undeniably authentic are all dramatic reversals of normal human presumptions. In this new order the poor, the hungry, the bereaved, the persecuted are congratulated.[53] In this new order people don't answer violence with violence; nor do they defend themselves against attempts to deprive them of their clothes – they'd rather walk around naked than offer such resistance. All the normal canons of prudent behaviour are being turned inside out. There is a lot of irony here, but something deeper than irony is also present. Jesus takes the measure of all normal expectations and reverses it: 'Love your enemies, do good to those who hate you, bless those who curse you, pray for those who abuse you. To him who strikes you on the cheek, offer the other also; and from him who takes away your coat do not withhold even your shirt.'

One of the most intriguing paradoxes of intellectual history is that it was a self-styled Antichrist who provided us with one of the best keys for understanding the psychology of Jesus. In *The Antichrist* Nietzsche described Jesus as an idiot;[54] but he was not going out of his way to insult him; he was, in fact, echoing Dostoevsky's great novel of that name, whose hero, a holy fool called Prince Myshkin, has a dangerously complicating effect on the lives of others.[55] I think Nietzsche is close to the mark here, though he doesn't quite hit it. The sense he gives is of an almost innocent naïvety in Jesus, like Alyosha in another Dostoevsky novel, *The Brothers Karamazov*; whereas I think something much more intentionally subversive is going on. The link lies in the contrast between the approach of Jesus and the kind of realpolitik of a world that is governed by the kind of force celebrated by Nietzsche as an undisguised expression of brutal reality. 'The essential characteristic of a good and healthy aristocracy is that it . . . accepts with a good conscience the sacrifice of untold human beings who, *for its sake*, must be reduced and lowered to incomplete human beings, to slaves, to instruments. Their fundamental faith simply has to be that society must not exist for society's sake but only as the foundation and scaffolding on which a choice type of being is able to raise itself to its higher task and to a higher state of being . . .'[56] Whether you want to enter or escape from this citadel of power, its main characteristic is its ruthless objectification of people, something Nietzsche well understood and brazenly celebrated in that passage from *Beyond Good and Evil*. Simone Weil was another subversive holy idiot with an interesting attitude to power. In an essay on the *Iliad*, which she described as the 'poem of force', she offered this definition: 'To define power or force – it is that X that turns anybody who is subjected to it into a thing.'[57] It is significant that these words were written by a woman, because the experience of objectification, of being turned into a thing, has been a constant element in woman's relationship with a world that has always been controlled by male power. It is also significant that one of the most consistent elements in the Jesus tradition is his sympathy for female victims of the domination system of his time. And his sympathy was not limited to female victims. Jesus belonged to a section of humanity that was even worse off than those Nietzsche described as slaves or instruments. In order to sustain the power citadel of the world of Jesus' day there had to be thousands of human instruments who existed to provide scaffolding for those who enjoyed life at the top. Nevertheless, everyone in the pyramid, even the ones who bore the pressure at the bottom, were maintained by and were therefore implicated in the system. Jesus identified himself with the people who were not in the system at all. These were the expendable class, the destitute; those with no leverage in the world; those who had no status or locus in organized human culture.[58] Jesus congratulates them ironically for being destitute and persecuted; for being outside all the systems of custom and law; for being victims of not participants in the world's systems of power. Since these systems all created victims, anyone implicated in them was guilty of the objectification that Simone Weil described: only the destitute, those absolutely excluded from power, could therefore be said to be innocent. John Dominic Crossan creates an ironic parody of the beatitudes from the beginning of the Sermon on the Mount, the better to draw out their meaning:

> Only the destitute are innocent.
> Only those who have no bread have no fault.
> Only the wretched are guiltless.
> Only the despised are blameless.[59]

One clue to the social status of the Jesus movement lies in Crossan's statement that those who have no bread have no fault. These are people who, far from having a place in the economic community, however lowly, are completely outside it, and have to beg for bread each day. This is the most likely meaning of the famous phrase in the Lord's Prayer, familiarly but misleadingly translated, 'Give us this day our daily bread'. The clause is a plea to find sufficient bread for the day, enough to survive another twenty-four hours. 'Daily' was translated misleadingly by the Greek word *epiousion*, an awkward word that might be paraphrased as 'enough to get by on, sufficient': *Give us enough bread for today* – the prayer of expendable people everywhere. And Jesus drives the subversive irony of the beatitudes further when he urges the community of the dispossessed, in their excluded world, not to mirror the customs of the included, with their ownership of property and the violence required to protect it: possessing nothing, they need defend nothing.

Behind the irony of Jesus' celebration of his people's complete lack of economic status there lies a deeper, more principled rejection of power. Jesus the holy fool, the subversive clown, belonged to that tiny but cleansing minority in human history who refuse to play the power game in any of its forms. He would have relished the irony that many of the most brutal power struggles of the last two millennia have been fought in his name. If we must categorize him at all, he is probably best understood as belonging to the artistic community rather than to the political community; and by political community I mean humanity in its organized forms, including its religious systems. There are always a few members of the human race who find themselves either by temperament or choice outside society's formal structures, which include the family and tribe, as well as all religious systems and political parties. These outlaws are ontologically incapable of the necessary but corrupting compromises required of those who participate in or broker between the powerful interest groups of organized society. To follow a Scottish usage, they choose to be 'outwith' the organized community. Since they are not implicated in the world's necessary arrangements, they bring purity as well as compassionate understanding to their reading of its workings.

The great novelists are probably the supreme example of this kind of transcendent perspective. We find a similar critical sympathy in Jesus: and its effect is to expose us to the social and psychological determinants of our actions, in both their personal and collective forms.

Though he did not discuss these issues in the abstract, his parables, as well as the company he kept, spelled the message out clearly. Jesus well understood that the necessity of law originates in our fear of the chaos of our own passions; but fear is a treacherous leader. He noticed that it was those who had the tightest control over their passions who risked the kind of emotional repression that resulted in cruelty to the morally frail. That was why he was loved by those who were victimized by their own weaknesses: he saw in them a generosity of spirit that was closer to the extravagant nature of God than the anxious carefulness of the highly disciplined. One of his parables was about a man who cravenly buried his master's money rather than risk its loss by venturing it. A similar tension re-appears in the Parable of the Prodigal Son, where the excesses of the profligate brother do not finally prevent him from responding to the love of the welcoming father; whereas the tightly coiled nature of the older brother may be the very thing that inhibits him from understanding the helplessness of the father's love, a point that is never resolved in the story, because it is left for us to finish.[60]

The human predicament is that we shuttle between excess and deprivation in our self-management. Controlled societies and individuals certainly achieve order in their lives, but the price they pay can be the stifling of the passions that enable us to transcend the narrowness of our lives. Even worse is when we end up condemning in others what we secretly long for in our own hearts. This dance between fascination and fear is an

ancient theme in all human systems. It accounts for the peri-
odic frenzies of internal persecution that mar the human story,
such as the purges of witches and heretics that disfigure
Christian history. Jesus knew that the human need for order
could operate as a cloak for spiritual cruelties that were ugly
substitutes for real passion. Implicit in his denunciation of
legalism was the recognition that passionate sinners were often
in better touch with their real nature than those who had
buried it beneath the law. However, the motive for this kind
of repression is understandable, because disordered humanity
is capable of terrifying excess. The thing to remember is that
the systems we create to contain our excesses can themselves
become excessive, so they require the constant criticism of the
prophetic imagination. A balanced life, recognizing the goodness of both passion and order, would establish a pattern of
directed passion. We would not kill off our nature and its
force, but nor would we allow it to dominate and drive us to
excess. One way of achieving this is through self-knowledge,
the kind of knowledge that knows the truth of its own desires
and speaks them honestly in its heart. The persecuting mind
never does this: which is why it lies to itself about its own
longings and then crucifies them in others.

Few of the followers of Jesus in history have been able to
maintain the kind of uncompromising compassion that is celebrated in the Sermon on the Mount. The Church itself,
which began as an outsider group in the Roman Empire, was
soon seduced by the attractions of power and, wherever it
established itself, learnt how to collude with it to its own
worldly benefit. But there has always been a radical element in
Christianity that has remained courageously loyal to the vision
of Jesus. You find these radical disciples everywhere – in
African shanty towns and South American barrios, American

urban ghettos and British sump housing estates – identifying themselves cheerfully with the dispossessed, and courageously challenging the systems that stunt and oppress them. Poor in spirit and pure in heart, they keep alive the challenge of Jesus to the thoughtless excesses of the powers that rule the world, proving that the Sermon on the Mount is still one of the most subversive utterances in history.

8

PARABLE

Luke [10:25] Just then a lawyer stood up to test Jesus. 'Teacher,' he said, 'what must I do to inherit eternal life?' [26] He said to him, 'What is written in the law? What do you read there?' [27] He answered, 'You shall love the Lord your God with all your heart, and with all your soul, and with all your strength, and with all your mind; and your neighbour as yourself.' [28] And he said to him, 'You have given the right answer; do this, and you will live.'

[29] But wanting to justify himself, he asked Jesus, 'And who is my neighbour?' [30] Jesus replied, 'A man was going down from Jerusalem to Jericho, and fell into the hands of robbers, who stripped him, beat him, and went away, leaving him half dead. [31] Now by chance a priest was going down that road; and when he saw him, he passed by on the other side. [32] So likewise a Levite, when he came to the place and saw him, passed by on the other side. [33] But a Samaritan while travelling came near him; and when he saw him, he was moved with pity. [34] He went to him and bandaged his wounds, having poured oil and wine on them. Then he put him on his own animal, brought him to an inn, and took care of him. [35] The next day he took out two denarii, gave them to the innkeeper, and said, "Take care of him; and when I come back, I will repay you whatever more you spend." [36] Which of these three, do you think, was a neighbour to the man who fell into the hands of the robbers?' [37] He said, 'The one who showed him mercy.' Jesus said to him, 'Go and do likewise.'

In this, his most famous parable, Jesus shows us how passion can be a better moral tutor than loyalty to established order. Before looking at it, let me offer a word of explanation about how I propose to handle it. One of the paradoxes about Jesus is the number of books that have been written about one who himself wrote nothing. He belongs to the oral tradition, a form of which he was clearly a master. The Scottish novelist James Kelman has coined the word *orature* to distinguish his kind of writing from *literature*. The best way to read a Kelman novel is to hear it. The paradox of his work is that it is speaking in writing. The same is true of Jesus. And something else needs to be said: the best words about Jesus are themselves usually spoken not written, which is why one of the most interesting theological genres is storytelling. The gospels tell us that Jesus spoke in *parables*, a word from the Greek for 'casting' or 'throwing over', the way a cowboy lassoes a steer by throwing the rope over its head to pull it in. A parable pulls the listener towards a new idea, usually a disturbing and surprising one. In discussing the parable of the Good Samaritan I want to try to be faithful to the oral tradition by giving it more of the cadence of orature than of literature: I want it to be heard rather than read. Perverse, I know, because, if you are still with me, you'll turn the page and keep on reading: I just hope you'll *hear* what is written.

The parable of the Good Samaritan is arguably the most famous short story in history: which is precisely its problem. Even people who have never read the text have a hazy idea of what it contains. The good Samaritan has become a generic example of selfless goodness, and there is even an organization, famous for helping the troubled, which is called after him. Most people will have heard and used the phrase, 'pass by on the other side', as an example of the kind of callous hypocrisy they think is characteristic of religion: 'These people,' they think, 'who profess one thing and do another – what hypocrites.' Once a text is in written form it takes on a life of its own, which is why it is pointless to rail against the varied readings that a good story elicits. The fact that the kind of daring neighbourliness shown by the Samaritan is commended by this story is all to the good: but I think it actually misses the main point of the parable, and the underlying attitude that Jesus was getting at. That is why the first thing we ought to do is discount the context in which Luke frames the story. He has taken a conversation found originally in Mark, the earliest gospel, and used it to answer the riddle of the Samaritan. In Mark 12:28–34, Jesus is asked by an expert in Jewish law which is the greatest commandment. In reply, he quotes the summary of the law: love God and love your neighbour as yourself. In Mark the scholar congratulates Jesus on his answer, and the conversation ends there. Luke spins the story on, by adding another question from the scholar: but who is my neighbour? This is Luke's way of defining the parable as a good example story; which is why he adds an admonition from Jesus to go and do likewise. But was that the original intention of Jesus? Was Jesus just telling his listeners to practise what they preached? It seems too pat and obvious to me; and Jesus was never pat and rarely obvious. To uncover the shock at the heart of the story we need to dig into the background rather than simply offer the most obvious surface reading, however improving it may be. The thing I want to claim at the outset is that this little narrative is not about the dangers of insincere religion; it is about the dangers of sincere religion. It is not about the pitfalls of religious hypocrisy; it is about the pitfalls of religious fidelity. That's the kick in the story, its main point, though there is nothing to stop us from doing a bit of allegorical extemporizing here and there, and the trail from Jerusalem to Jericho is a good place to start.

This is still a winding, foreboding road that gives off an air of menace. It snakes its way through an arid landscape of the sort familiar to addicts of Hollywood Westerns: prime territory for ambushes and hold-ups, the kind of place where the solitary traveller would be anxious about what might be waiting for him round the next bend. I have driven it several times in solid motor vehicles, but I wouldn't fancy footing it, even if I were heavily loaded with bottled water and had an armed escort. It is no surprise that down the centuries preachers have allegorized the road and seen it as a parable of life's journey. It is on this road we catch sight of a solitary figure, almost certainly understood by the original audience to be a Jew, and probably a poor one like themselves, someone they can identify with. They are already keyed up by the opening: Mr Everyman is hurrying along nightmare alley, and the inevitable happens. The thugs who jump him not only rob him and beat him senseless, they strip him naked and leave him for dead by the side of the road.

Next along the road comes a priest, and this is where we have to pause and reflect. By this time the original hearers had probably anticipated the outline of the story and its expected denouement, so we can think of them smiling scornfully as the priest ambles onto the scene, probably riding a donkey. Priests belonged to both the spiritual and the economic aristocracy of Israel. The priests of the Jerusalem temple were a privileged caste, and the temple itself was a major economic resource for the area. It was not only the spiritual centre of Judaism – Mecca and Vatican City rolled into one – its flourishing sacrifice system was the main staple of the local economy. As Robert Funk explains: 'The importance of the cult for the economic well-being of Jerusalem cannot be over-estimated. Herds and flocks were in constant demand for sacrificial offerings, and the influx of pilgrims at festival times required money changing and banking.'[61] Human nature being what it is, we can easily imagine the opportunity all this provided for feathering nests, favouring relatives and exploit-ing the poor. We can probably assume that his audience already knew that Jesus was a critic of the temple cult,[62] and we can also take for granted in them an agreeable level of anti-clericalism of the sort that is universally present among the bolshier elements of peasant societies. The temple priests and their Levites – lay assistants who were responsible for the temple's liturgical infrastructure, such as music, incense, sacred bread, as well as the temple curtains and adornments[63] – had quarters in the Jordan valley near Jericho to which they retreated as often as they could.[64] Wending their separate ways, these two were probably off for a few days' holiday after an intense period of duty in the temple.

What can we know about them? Obviously nothing per-sonal, but we know a lot about their religious and social world. Its main characteristic was fear of ritual defilement, the flip side of a positive quest for purity. In the larger world with which they interacted there were many opportunities for defilement, some of them avoidable, some of them not; all of them necessitating rituals of purification that were time con-suming and often required professional priestly assistance. The positive side of the code was that a sacred space was available to them, an inside world of temple and holy day, that reflected the transcendent purity of God, whose perfection they were called to imitate. The negative side of the code was that there was an outside world that was loaded with multitudinous opportunities for defilement, from unclean races, unclean foods, unclean fluids such as semen and menstrual blood, the wrong kind of material woven into clothing, diseases of the skin, and dead bodies. Coming into contact with any of these sources of pollution caused a form of ritual defilement that precluded the contaminated person from participation in the temple cult, as well as from social contact with others who were themselves in a state of ritual purity.[65] It is important to understand that we are talking about ritual not ethical defilement, a distinction that may be difficult for a modern reader to grasp. The distinction between dirt and immorality may capture the difference. Dirt has been described as matter out of place: marmalade on your toast is good; marmalade on your tie is not; there, it's dirt. Now, you may feel scruffy with a dirty tie, but you do not feel immoral: all you need to do is wipe it off. Ritual impurity was a bit like that. It was an impersonal force, a sort of radioactive staining; but its consequential effects could be profoundly damaging to people, especially if they belonged to an unclean profession, such as tax-farming, or were in a permanent state of impurity because they did not have the wherewithal to achieve purification, which was the position occupied by the expendable class Jesus identified with. Seeking purification after defilement could be complex or straightforward; some of it you could do at home; some of it required a visit to the temple. And for some, there was nothing they could do about it, because of the immutability of their excluded state.

This was the code that defined the lives of the priest and the Levite who were on their way from Jerusalem to Jericho the day our traveller fell among thieves. The purity code was the defining characteristic of their lives and it required from them a permanent and vigorous state of psychological engagement. As I have already pointed out, we know nothing of the personal lives of these men, but we should not jump too quickly to condemn the complexity of a religious system that is alien to our own consciousness. Even religions that baffle us deserve the benefit of the doubt, and so should this priest as he wrestles with the predicament that confronts him when he turns the corner and sees a naked man lying on the other side of the road. Given the intricate and encompassing nature of his religious commitment, spontaneity was out of the question for him: he had to perform a complex spiritual calculus in order to plan his response. Apart from the physical risk involved in hanging around such a dangerous spot, his main anxiety would be the threat the unknown man presented to his state of ritual purity. Was he dead? It was impossible to tell from this distance: if he gets close enough to verify his state and discovers he is dead, the priest will be immediately defiled: no three-day break for him in the Jordan valley where his family is eagerly anticipating his arrival. It is back to the temple to cleanse himself. And if he is alive, what if he turns out to belong to an unclean people like the hated Samaritans? Touch him, come into contact with his blood, and it is the same story. Prudence wins, as it often does in the religious calculus. He shakes his head, kicks his heels into the donkey's flanks, and trots past on the other side. The chances are that the Levite, next on the scene, has seen his superior up ahead and witnessed his decision to ride on. He is not going to second-guess the boss but, being a conscientious man, he too makes the calculation, and comes to the same conclusion. He also passes by on the other side at a safe ritual distance. Scoff if you must, but this is not moral hypocrisy; it is a justifiable decision, given the internal logic of the religious system followed by both men. The audience is not surprised.

They saw it coming. It is what they expected. They know the system, and some of them would have done the same.

No surprises so far; but one is just about to appear. As far as the audience is concerned, the symmetry of the story requires the next person on the scene to be an ordinary Israelite, the little man, someone who did not come from the priestly elite or its hangers-on: Priest, Levite, Israelite, that is the order. And it turns out to be a Samaritan! The Samaritans were despised by Jews as an unclean bastard race, descendants of Israelites who had stayed behind when the leading families were deported to Assyria after the conquest of 722 BCE. They had intermarried with foreign settlers, transplanted by the Assyrians into their new colony.[66] In spite of their excluded status, the Samaritans continued to observe the Torah; they had even built their own temple on Mount Gerizim, which was destroyed by the Israelites in the first century BCE, thereby exacerbating the enmity between the two groups. Their running conflict is an icon of the sort of ethnic hatreds that are wearyingly familiar in human history, such as the volcanic hatred between Serbs and Croats or the feuding communities in Northern Ireland today.

Anyway, round the bend it is a Samaritan who comes next, and a prosperous one by the look of him. Though he is a ritual and social enemy of the priest and Levite who preceded him to this spot, he too follows the Torah, he too is committed to the purity code, he too runs the same risks of defilement. Surely he will make the same calculation and pass prudently by on the other side? But no: something else happens, something shattering. Unfortunately, our English translation does not capture the explosive nature of the event: it tells us that 'he was moved with pity', but that phrase does not catch the power of his reaction. The Greek verb at the heart of the story is *esplanknise* (verse 33) and behind it lies a neuter plural noun *ta splankna*, meaning entrails or bowels. It is a powerful word: at the sight of the naked and bleeding man at the roadside the Samaritan's guts churned inside him with such ferocity that it simply obliterated the purity code. The passion of his pity for a fellow human blew down the walls that ritually separated him from a supposed enemy.

This deceptively simple story encapsulates Jesus' attitude to the spiritual and moral danger we are in when we allow our codes and traditions to assume absolute authority over us. It is true that we need moral and religious systems to protect us from the chaos of our passions; but if we give them transcendent and unchanging authority they become a greater danger to us than the unfettered passions they are supposed to curb. An unalterable code can close us against ordinary pity for our fellows, and cause us to treat them not as humans, but as abstractions, as things. When this happens to our consciousness we render ourselves incapable of meeting others on the human level, our own level: instead, we encounter them as objects, whether religious or political. By this parable, and by his ironic attitude to the rigidities of law and custom, Jesus rendered every code provisional and discardable when the circumstances required it. A modern example of the danger of undeviating moral rigidity is provided by Catholicism's absolute prohibition on the use of artificial contraceptive devices during sexual intercourse. The ban on contraception is part of their religious commitment, and if you buy the moral theory you buy the practice. But if you apply the code unyieldingly in the context of the AIDS pandemic in Africa, for instance, and absolutely forbid the use of condoms in all circumstances, you are acquiescing in the needless deaths of millions of people. Your moral code, good as it may be in the right context, is the very thing that is holding you back from crossing the Jericho road and going to the assistance of the man who has fallen among thieves. To be fair to Luke, he understood this message better than Matthew did. We have already noted Matthew's ambivalence to Jesus' radicalism: he couldn't quite bring himself to accept the unnerving consequences of according human codes such a conditional status in a world that craved moral certainty. He swallowed hard and gave us hard-core Jesus only slightly modified; but he also gave us solid shots of the old law as well, ending with the great Levitical command to his readers to be perfect as their heavenly father was perfect. Luke saw what Jesus was really getting at: by the end of his version of the great sermon he realizes that we are called not to the impossibility of perfection, but to the possibility of compassion: 'Be compassionate, even as your Father is compassionate.'[67] The meaning of the parable of the Good Samaritan is that it is compassion, not code, that is the basis for a truly universal human ethic.

9

APOSTLE

Acts of the Apostles [9:1] Meanwhile Saul, still breathing threats and murder against the disciples of the Lord, went to the high priest [2] and asked him for letters to the synagogues at Damascus, so that if he found any who belonged to the Way, men or women, he might bring them bound to Jerusalem. [3] Now as he was going along and approaching Damascus, suddenly a light from heaven flashed around him. [4] He fell to the ground and heard a voice saying to him, 'Saul, Saul, why do you persecute me?' [5] He asked, 'Who are you, Lord?' The reply came, 'I am Jesus, whom you are persecuting. [6] But get up and enter the city, and you will be told what you are to do.' [7] The men who were travelling with him stood speechless because they heard the voice but saw no one. [8] Saul got up from the ground, and though his eyes were open, he could see nothing; so they led him by the hand and brought him into Damascus. [9] For three days he was without sight, and neither ate nor drank.

[10] Now there was a disciple in Damascus named Ananias. The Lord said to him in a vision, 'Ananias.' He answered, 'Here I am, Lord.' [11] The Lord said to him, 'Get up and go to the street called Straight, and at the house of Judas look for a man of Tarsus named Saul. At this moment he is praying, [12] and he has seen in a vision a man named Ananias come in and lay his hands on him so that he might regain his sight.' [13] But Ananias answered, 'Lord, I have heard from many about this man, how much evil he has done to your saints in Jerusalem; [14] and here he has authority from the chief

priests to bind all who invoke your name.' [15] But the Lord said to him, 'Go, for he is an instrument whom I have chosen to bring my name before Gentiles and kings and before the people of Israel; [16] I myself will show him how much he must suffer for the sake of my name.' [17] So Ananias went and entered the house. He laid his hands on Saul and said, 'Brother Saul, the Lord Jesus, who appeared to you on your way here, has sent me so that you may regain your sight and be filled with the Holy Spirit.' [18] And immediately something like scales fell from his eyes, and his sight was restored. Then he got up and was baptized, [19] and after taking some food, he regained his strength.

For several days he was with the disciples in Damascus, [20] and immediately he began to proclaim Jesus in the synagogues, saying, 'He is the Son of God.' [21] All who heard him were amazed and said, 'Is not this the man who made havoc in Jerusalem among those who invoked this name? And has he not come here for the purpose of bringing them bound before the chief priests?' [22] Saul became increasingly more powerful and confounded the Jews who lived in Damascus by proving that Jesus was the Messiah.

Jesus and Paul are the good cop, bad cop of Christianity. Whereas people are usually reluctant to criticize Jesus, Paul has always had a legion of detractors, both within and without the Christian movement. This has something to do with the inevitable loss of innocence that follows the institutional consolidation of any charismatic movement. The second generation, the generation that consolidates the original vision into some sort of institutional continuity, is invariably compared unflatteringly with the passion of the founder. It was Paul, the persecutor turned convert, whose energetic genius secured the future of Christianity, but what was lost in the process, and how true was he to the radical vision of Jesus? These are the questions that continue to haunt the reputation of the great Apostle Paul. With characteristic immoderation, Nietzsche sums up the case against him:

That the ship of Christianity threw overboard a good deal of its Jewish ballast, that it went, and was able to go, among the pagans – that was due to this one man, a very tortured, very pitiful, very unpleasant man, unpleasant even to himself. He suffered from a fixed idea – or more precisely, from a fixed, ever-present, never resting question: what about the Jewish law? and particularly the fulfilment of this law? In his youth he had himself wanted to satisfy it, with a ravenous hunger for this highest distinction which the Jews could conceive – this people who were propelled higher than any other people by the imagination of the ethically sublime, and who alone succeeded in creating a holy god together with the idea of sin as a transgression against this holiness. Paul became the fanatical defender of this god and his law and guardian of his honour; at the same time, in the struggle against the transgressors and doubters, lying in wait for them, he became increasingly harsh and evilly disposed to them, and inclined toward the most extreme punishments. And now found that – hot-headed, sensual, melancholy, malignant in his hatred as he was – he was himself unable to fulfil the law: indeed, and this seemed strangest to him, his extravagant lust to domineer provoked him continually to transgress the law, and he had to yield to this thorn.

Nietzsche then went on to offer another penetrating insight:

The law was the cross to which he felt himself nailed: how he hated it! how he resented it! how he searched for some means to annihilate it – not to fulfil it any more himself! And finally the saving thought struck him, together with a vision – it could scarcely have happened otherwise to this epileptic . . . Paul heard the words: 'Why dost thou persecute me?' The essential occurrence, however, was this: his head had suddenly seen a light: 'It is unreasonable,' he had said to himself, 'to persecute this Jesus! Here after all is the way out; here is the perfect revenge; here and nowhere else I have and hold the annihilator of the law.' Until then the ignominious death had seemed to him the chief argument against the Messianic claim of which the adherents of the new doctrine spoke: but what if it were necessary to get rid of the law?'[68]

Analysing and reinterpreting the case for the prosecution is one way to mount a defence, so I'll come back to Nietzsche's speech to the jury when I take a look at the theological ideas Paul developed: meanwhile I want to sketch in the few facts we have about his history. Everything we know about him we get from the New Testament, the only primary source, either from the Acts of the Apostles – the second volume of Luke's account of the Christian movement – or from Paul's own letters. We have already noted that the gospels are better understood as theological rather than as historical narratives, and the same has to be said of Acts. In marked contrast to the turbulent account found in Paul's letters, Acts gives us an idealized version of the struggle to open up the Christian movement to Gentiles. However, it is the only source we have for establishing the outlines of Paul's biography, and there is no reason to doubt the accuracy of the few facts it gives us. It is from Acts that we learn Paul was born into a Jewish family in Tarsus in Cilicia; that his Hebrew name was Saul; that he was trained in rabbinic studies in Jerusalem under a legendary scholar called Gamaliel; that he was a Roman citizen; that he was a tentmaker by trade and continued to work at it when he became a Christian missionary; that after a period of intense hatred of the Christian movement, he had a dramatic conversion to it.[69] The only independently attested date we have for him comes from a story in Acts 18, where we read that, 'When Gallio was proconsul of Achaia, the Jews made a united attack upon Paul and brought him before the tribunal.' Gallio was proconsul in 51–2 CE. The other date on offer comes from an early legend that Paul was beheaded in Rome about 65 CE.

So much for the sketchy biographical outline. We are on much more solid ground when we come to his correspondence, though it is not as abundant as the attributions in the New Testament assert. Of the thirteen letters attributed to Paul only seven are accepted as absolutely authentic by most scholars, though a few of the other six are argued over. The indisputably authentic letters are Romans, I and II Corinthians, Galatians, Philippians, I Thessalonians, and Philemon; II Thessalonians and Colossians are disputed, some scholars giving them the nod, others the thumbs down. Ephesians, though it is heavy with Pauline vocabulary and theology, is reckoned by some scholars to be later than Paul. And everyone agrees that what are called the Pastoral epistles, Titus and I and II Timothy, are much later and reflect a more developed stage of early Christianity. While the genuine letters offer independent attestation of his hatred of Christianity before his conversion, it is their theological content that is important, because it marks the first stage in a long doctrinal development that reached its apogee in 325 CE at the Council of Nicaea, when Jesus was definitively pronounced to be God the Son, one in being with God the Father. So Paul is fundamental to the evolution of Christology, the study of the person of Jesus in relationship to God. What is more easily overlooked is that, though he never alludes to it, Paul is as interested in the teaching of the human Jesus as in his status as the divine redeemer sent by God to save the world. His attitude to the Torah, the great project of the Jewish code, could be read as an explicit formalizing of the attitude of Jesus to the temple cult and its purity code. The main difficulty that confronts untutored readers of the Bible is that, because of the way the books are sequenced in the New Testament, it is logical to assume that the gospels came first and Paul and his letters came at the end. In fact, the right order is:

a) what scholars call the life of the historical Jesus – as opposed to what they call, because it emerged after decades of reflection, 'the Christ of faith';

b) the development of the oral tradition that carried the remembrance of him after his death in the early Christian movement;

c) Paul's eruption into that movement, with his passionate re-interpretation of Jesus Christ as the saviour sent by God to complete the work begun by Israel and transfigure Christianity into a universal faith;

d) his struggle to have his re-interpretation accepted by the leaders of the Church, leading eventually to his mission to convert the Gentiles, without requiring their submission to the Jewish code;

e) his relentless missionary work, reflected in the letters he wrote to his converts, working out the theological and ecclesiastical consequences of the new order he was establishing;

f) his death, probably around 65 CE in Rome;

g) the first written gospel, almost certainly Mark's, appearing a few years after Paul's death, to be followed by the others during the next three or four decades;

h) the Church in Jerusalem was the section of the Christian movement that was most opposed to Paul's radical programme of opening up the movement to the Gentiles, but even it gradually separated itself from Judaism in the years following the destruction of the Temple by the Romans in 70 CE.

Depending on how these developments are viewed, Pauline theology is held to be either the necessary first stage in the development of Christianity from a messianic movement within Judaism into a universal church; or it is dismissed as a pure invention of Paul, the first Christian – though there is no reason why it couldn't be both. But it is time now to turn to the man and his ideas, by turning to Nietzsche's central accusation that historical Christianity owes more to Paul's tortured psychology than to the Jewish radicalism of Jesus.

Paul was 'a very tortured, very pitiful, very unpleasant man, unpleasant even to himself'. Paul would probably have agreed with that character sketch, certainly with the tortured bit. He tells us in his letter to Galatians that in his former life in Judaism he had persecuted the young Jesus movement violently and tried to destroy it. He also tells us that he had advanced in Judaism beyond many his own age and was a zealot on behalf of its traditions.[70] The key word there, *zelotes*, has a certain ambiguity about it: it can mean one who is zealous, or one who is a Zealot, a member of a nationalistic sect. However we translate the word, the psychology is interesting. Bertrand Russell said that zeal was a bad mark for a cause, because it always betrayed the presence of inner doubt. We could say of this very tortured man that he found it impossible to be moderate about anything, because he was always struggling with his own demons. After all, it is one thing to be a devout Jew; it is quite another to feel compelled to persecute those who disagree with you. Yet it is usually the immoderates who push for those changes in human affairs that alter the course of history, and that is certainly what happened here. Without Paul Christianity would probably have maintained a shadowy existence within Judaism for a generation or two as a tiny cult, before disappearing from history like other sects that had formed themselves round messianic pretenders in the past. So, whatever we think of him and the body he founded, we owe a debt of gratitude to Paul for creating a movement that preserved the memory and words of Jesus.

Jung thought that the blindness that struck Paul the persecutor on the road to Damascus was of a piece with his inner torment. There are none as blind as those who will not see, and there was clearly a great struggle going on in the zealot who was determined to stamp out the memory of the man who so painfully haunted his consciousness. Though there is no record of his ever having seen Jesus, it is impossible to believe that Paul had not heard of the refusal of Jesus to accord absolute and unconditional authority to any human code, even one as revered as the Torah. Nietzsche was right in putting his finger here in his analysis of Paul's struggle: he himself was unable to fulfil the very law he revered. And this struggle continued after his conversion to Christianity. He was always a divided man, longing for a perfection he could not achieve by his own efforts: 'I do not understand my own actions. For I do not do what I want, but I do the very thing I hate.'[71] Blinded by the obduracy of his own predicament, it suddenly struck him that Jesus was right about code and cult. Nietzsche makes the transaction sound psychologically dubious: Paul hates himself for being unable to keep the law; he projects that self-hatred onto the followers of one who sat lightly to the law; but he is finally rescued from his predicament and achieves integration by going over to the side of the annihilator of the law. That sequence may capture something of the psychological complexity of Paul's conversion, but it is just as likely that he was finally persuaded by Jesus' attitude to the cult, which was one of general but not unconditional acceptance. The human community needed codes of law and conduct to help restrain its proneness to chaos, but if they were allowed to become absolute and insisted on undeviating observance, they would destroy the very purpose they were meant to serve, which was the good of humanity. 'The Sabbath was made for humanity, not humanity for the Sabbath.'[72] It is also important to recognize that Paul made a fundamental distinction between the moral and the ritual elements of the law. While Christians were now free of the ritual law – and need not circumcise their sons or eat kosher food –

they were not free to sin.[73] The fact that he had to point out this distinction to his converts suggests that they themselves did not fully grasp the finer points of his position. To Paul, the full panoply of the Torah, its ritual as well as its moral prescriptions, had been created to prepare the way for the coming of the Lord. Now that he had appeared, the law had fulfilled its purpose like a midwife and could leave the scene with pride in a job well done. Whatever we make of the Pauline claim, it undoubtedly became the foundation on which the universal Church was built. By maintaining the moral discipline and seriousness of Judaism, while abrogating its more awkward ritual requirements, Paul guaranteed a successful future for the Church in the fertile field of Gentile evangelism.

In order to discuss Paul's theological ideas we have to divide them into separate elements, though that inevitably distorts what is essentially a package deal. At the heart of Paul's conversion, and the ideas that flowed consequentially from it, there lay a mystical encounter with the spirit of the crucified Galilean. Whether we offer a natural or supernatural reading of this event, it was the source from which everything else streamed. In the jargon of theologians, his conversion was an eschatological event: it was a vision of the imminent completion of all things and the final coming of God's reign. Even his repudiation of the Torah is eschatological. It has served its purpose and been replaced by the living spirit of Jesus:

Romans [8:1] There is therefore now no condemnation for those who are in Christ Jesus. [2] For the law of the Spirit of life in Christ Jesus has set you free from the law of sin and of death. [3] For God has done what the law, weakened by the flesh, could not do: by sending his own Son in the likeness of sinful flesh, and to deal with sin, he condemned sin in the flesh, [4] so that the just requirement of the law might be fulfilled in us, who walk not according to the flesh but according to the Spirit. [5] For those who live according to the flesh set their minds on the things of the flesh, but those who live according to the Spirit set their minds on the things of the Spirit. [6] To set the mind on the flesh is death, but to set the mind on the Spirit is life and peace. [7] For this reason the mind that is set on the flesh is hostile to God; it does not submit to God's law – indeed it cannot, [8] and those who are in the flesh cannot please God.

[9] But you are not in the flesh; you are in the Spirit, since the Spirit of God dwells in you. Anyone who does not have the Spirit of Christ does not belong to him. [10] But if Christ is in you, though the body is dead because of sin, the Spirit is life because of righteousness. [11] If the Spirit of him who raised Jesus from the dead dwells in you, he who raised Christ from the dead will give life to your mortal bodies also through his Spirit that dwells in you.

What the old law could not achieve, because of the weakness of human nature, God now does for those who have been mystically incorporated into the life of the crucified yet living saviour. In view of the lateness of the hour and the closeness of the Second Coming of Christ, God has foreshortened the process of redemption into one of dramatic immediacy. This was the flash of insight that suddenly blinded Saul the persecutor on his violent mission to Damascus. Once light illumined his darkened mind, he realized there was no time to lose. The end of all things would soon come through the agency of the one who had appeared to him.[74] In the time left to this dying world, it was the mission of the Church to call people to salvation by submitting to the Lord Jesus before his return in judgment, when it would be too late to escape the wrath of God.[75] It is the eschatological imperative that accounts for the urgency and dynamism of Paul's missionary work among the Gentiles. In the febrile religious atmosphere of his time, he planted outposts of the Christian movement in the strategic centres of the Roman Empire's provinces in Asia Minor, and at the end of his life he brought the message to Rome itself. The last seven chapters of the Acts of the Apostles close Paul's ministry with a sort of paradoxical symmetry. It was from Jerusalem that Paul had set out, 'breathing threats and murder', in pursuit of the disciples of Jesus. And it was in Jerusalem, on his final visit many years later, that he was saved from lynching by the very community he had once served, when the Roman authorities took him into custody for his own protection. After a sequence of trials before both the Jewish and Roman authorities, invoking his Roman citizenship, Paul appealed to Caesar and to Caesar, or at least to Rome, he was sent. He arrived there probably about 60 CE,[76] and remained under house arrest for two years. There the record ends, though legend has it that he was beheaded in 65 CE. Whatever we make of his theology, there is something undoubtedly noble and moving about the thought of this old man, worn out by the urgency of his mission, and wearing the chains of captivity, bringing the gospel to Rome itself. The rest, as we say, without exaggeration in this case, is history.

10

END

Revelation [20:1] Then I saw an angel coming down from heaven, holding in his hand the key to the bottomless pit and a great chain. [2] He seized the dragon, that ancient serpent, who is the Devil and Satan, and bound him for a thousand years, [3] and threw him into the pit, and locked and sealed it over him, so that he would deceive the nations no more, until the thousand years were ended. After that he must be let out for a little while.

[4] Then I saw thrones, and those seated on them were given authority to judge. I also saw the souls of those who had been beheaded for their testimony to Jesus and for the word of God. They had not worshipped the beast or its image and had not received its mark on their foreheads or their hands. They came to life and reigned with Christ for a thousand years. [5] (The rest of the dead did not come to life until the thousand years were ended.) This is the first resurrection. [6] Blessed and holy are those who share in the first resurrection. Over these the second death has no power, but they will be priests of God and of Christ, and they will reign with him for a thousand years.

[7] When the thousand years are ended, Satan will be released from his prison [8] and will come out to deceive the nations at the four corners of the earth, Gog and Magog, in order to gather them for battle; they are as numerous as the sands of the sea. [9] They marched up over the breadth of the earth and surrounded the camp of the saints and the beloved city. And fire came down from heaven

and consumed them. [10] And the devil who had deceived them was thrown into the lake of fire and sulphur, where the beast and the false prophet were, and they will be tormented day and night for ever and ever.

[11] Then I saw a great white throne and the one who sat on it; the earth and the heaven fled from his presence, and no place was found for them. [12] And I saw the dead, great and small, standing before the throne, and books were opened. Also another book was opened, the book of life. And the dead were judged according to their works, as recorded in the books. [13] And the sea gave up the dead that were in it, Death and Hades gave up the dead that were in them, and all were judged according to what they had done. [14] Then Death and Hades were thrown into the lake of fire. This is the second death, the lake of fire; [15] and anyone whose name was not found written in the book of life was thrown into the lake of fire.

The first word of the last book of the Bible is a compound made from the preposition *apo*, 'away from', and the substantive form of the verb *kalupto*, to 'hide' or 'cover': hence, *apokalupsis*, that which is 'uncovered', 'disclosed', 'revealed'. 'The revelation, *apokalupsis*, of Jesus Christ, which God gave him to show his servants what must soon take place; he made it known by sending his angel to his servant John, [2] who testified to the word of God and to the testimony of Jesus Christ, even to all that he saw.' We don't know who John was, though in early Christian tradition he was held to be the Apostle John, who had been exiled to the isle of Patmos[77] by Domitian, Roman Emperor from 81 to 96 CE. Roman historians classified Domitian as a tyrant, and Christian tradition as a persecutor of the young Church. The author of Revelation tells us that he was in a trance or, in his own words, 'in the Spirit' on the Lord's day, during a period of tribulation, when he heard a voice like a trumpet telling him to write down in a book what he was seeing and send it to the seven churches of Asia Minor.[78] These exhortations against backsliding and tepid discipleship are found in the first three chapters: it is not till chapter four that he really gets into his apocalyptic stride: [4:1] After this I looked, and there in heaven a door stood open! And the first voice, which I had heard speaking to me like a trumpet, said, 'Come up here, and I will show you what must take place after this.' [2] At once I was in the spirit, and there in heaven stood a throne, with one seated on the throne!

Early Christianity was an apocalyptic movement, living in daily expectation of the return of Christ, whose second advent would herald the end of the world. As we noted in the previous chapter, this was a dominant element in Paul's theological scheme, though its origins lie well back in the Hebrew scriptures. Apocalyptic expectation is a common theme in the history of beaten peoples, including the native communities of North America who faced US expansion into their historic homelands.[79] Apocalyptic longing is best thought of as an ultimate form of compensatory justice. If there is a belief in the providential care of God for a people whose actual historical experience is of woe and oppression, then it is not hard to figure out how passionate longing for a better future could project itself into the expectation of a supernatural eruption into history by God to avenge his children and establish justice on earth. The Jewish concept of messiah is itself an apocalyptic one, presaging the return of the once and future king who would restore the fortunes of Israel and inaugurate God's righteous reign on earth. It is impossible to subtract this eschatological theme from early Christian history. Though it clearly goes back to Jesus himself, scholars vary in their estimation of his own attitude to it. In his classic study of the subject, the ground-breaking *Quest of the Historical Jesus*, Albert Schweitzer became convinced that Jesus saw himself as a prophet of the imminent in-breaking of God into human history; but he died in despair because it did not occur:

> The apocalyptic movement in the time of Jesus is not connected with any historic event. It cannot be said that we know anything about the Messianic expectations of the Jewish people at that time. On the contrary, the indifference shown by the Roman administration towards the movement proves that the Romans knew nothing of a condition of great and general Messianic excitement among the Jewish people. What is really remarkable about this wave of apocalyptic enthusiasm (which grew from the work of the Baptist and Jesus) is the fact that it was called forth not by external events, but solely by the appearance of two great personalities, and subsides with their disappearance, without leaving among the people generally any trace, except a feeling of hatred towards the new sect. The Baptist and Jesus . . . set the times in motion by acting, by creating eschatological facts . . . There is silence all around. The Baptist appears, and cries: 'Repent, for the Kingdom of Heaven is at hand.' Soon after that comes Jesus, and in the knowledge that He is the coming Son of Man lays hold of the wheel of the world to set it moving on that last revolution which is to bring all ordinary history to a close. It refuses to turn, and He throws Himself upon it. Then it does turn; and crushes him. Instead of bringing in the eschatological conditions, He has destroyed them. The wheel rolls onward, and the mangled body of the one immeasurably great Man, who was strong enough to think of Himself as the spiritual ruler of mankind and to bend history to his purpose, is hanging upon it still.[80]

Though other scholars have disputed Schweitzer's claim that Jesus died in eschatological despair, the words spoken from the cross recorded in Mark, the earliest gospel, seems to support it: 'My God, my God, why have you forsaken me?'[81] Whatever view we take of the messianic consciousness of Jesus, the presence of an apocalyptic or predictive element in his teaching undoubtedly created a problem for the many generations of believers who were to follow him. Somewhere around 50 CE Paul tackled the issue of the delayed return of Jesus in his first letter, sent to some of his Thessalonian converts who were troubled by the fate of Christians who had already died: what would become of them at the end of the world? Paul, probably making it up as he went along, seems to be in no doubt:

> I Thessalonians [4:13] But we do not want you to be uninformed, brothers and sisters, about those who have died, so that you may not grieve as others do who have no hope. [14] For since we believe that Jesus died and rose again, even so, through Jesus, God will bring with him those who have died. [15] For this we declare to you by the word of the Lord, that we who are alive, who are left until the coming of the Lord, will by no means precede those who have died. [16] For the Lord himself, with a cry of command, with the archangel's call and with the sound of God's trumpet, will descend from heaven, and the dead in Christ will rise first. [17] Then we who are alive, who are left, will be caught up in the clouds together with them to meet the Lord in the air; and so we will be with the Lord for ever. [18] Therefore encourage one another with these words.

However, the problems of interpretation presented by the apocalyptic element in Jesus and Paul are nothing compared to the challenge presented by the spectacular visions of Revelation. At the time of its writing we are well into the early Christian era, probably somewhere around 95 CE. Paul was long dead, as were the other apostles, and the promised return of the Lord had still not happened. Is the unidentified John, seer of Patmos, looking through a glass darkly into the future, maybe even the distant future, and describing what is to come? Is Revelation an ordnance survey map of the end-time, enabling those who are good at eschatological orienteering to read the signs and locate their exact position in history with reference to its denouement? That has certainly been one of the main uses to which this exotic text has been put. The religious imagination in its more florid manifestations has had an unbridled lust for the promise or threat of spectacular eruptions of the supernatural into the natural order, and many of them have been fired by this book. One obvious element in the visions of Revelation is the eschatological significance of the millennium.

Millenarianism has been a prominent strand among radical Christian sects, though they have usually disagreed among themselves as to the precise timing of the thousand years of blessedness. Some believe that the thousand years of bliss will precede and prepare the way for the second Advent of Christ, others that it will follow after it. Throughout the history of the Church there have been numerous bouts of millennial fever, not always associated with that thousand-year click of the cosmic clock, though the ominous nature of that moment always brings millenarianists out of the woodwork. The advent of the second Christian millennium witnessed only a modest level of apocalyptic fervour, though it was reported that a group of American fundamentalists, hoping for a ringside seat at the second coming, camped out above the field of Armageddon outside Jerusalem, prompted by a verse in Revelation which gave it as a precise map reference for the final conflict.[82] Their disappointment is part of a long tradition of eschatological failure that never dents the confidence of those who read Revelation as a coded blueprint for the end-time. Failure to get the date right only serves to fortify their conviction that they haven't cracked the code accurately enough: understandable, after all, if you believe that the last book of the Bible is a profound riddle set by God to warn his elect about the great tribulation that is to come upon the earth. According to the American billionaire television evangelist Pat Robertson, it will definitely happen in 2007. It is easy to smile at this kind of thing, and see it as a bit of harmless fun, like the Y2K panic that hit the world's PC owners in 1999. But there is a more sinister side to contemporary versions of apocalyptic theorizing. It has become the peculiar preserve of the Christian Right in the USA, where it has morphed into a vast conspiracy theory that is now one of the most powerful and volatile weapons in America's increasingly strident culture wars. One of the leaders of the neo-apocalyptic movement, a writer who is hardly known outside the USA, Tim LaHaye, has been named by the *Evangelical Studies Bulletin* as the most influential Christian leader of the last quarter century, more influential even than Billy Graham. LaHaye is the co-author of the *Left Behind* series of novels about the end-time, which have sold more than 30 million copies through outlets such as Wal-Mart. LaHaye is part of the Christian Right that sees all around it a deadly conspiracy of prowling humanists, liberals and feminists, who are all out to destroy the family and eliminate Christian values from the USA. Descried through this apocalyptic prism, war, pestilence, famine and death – the four horsemen of the apocalypse – form a pattern that reveals the dreadful imminence of the end-time. Rather than look for ways to address the problems that beset the world, the apocalyptic mindset actually welcomes them as signs that the end is accelerating towards us. Jerry Falwell, a co-conspirator of LaHaye, when asked about the growing degradation of the planet, said he had no concern about it whatsoever. Jesus would be back soon to end the world, so we might as well use it before we lose it.[83] This is not a piece of harmless eschatological fun we can cheerfully ignore. It has become a rogue element in the political consciousness of the world's only superpower. There is evidence that it has had an influence on recent USA foreign policy; but even if that is denied, it has undoubtedly affected the political rhetoric of President Bush. The final irony will be if the apocalyptic conspiracy theory contributes to the end of the world not as a supernatural, but as a natural phenomenon, because it hinders the attempt to rescue the planet from the consequences of human folly. There is, after all, a respectable scientific version of apocalyptic that predicts the possible end of the world not as a consequence of divine anger, but as the result of human greed and indifference. That is why the sane and ferociously well-informed Astronomer Royal of Britain, Martin Rees, has given his book, *Our Final Century*, a subtitle that could have been lifted from the pages of Revelation: *A scientist's warning: how terror, error, and environmental disaster threaten humankind's future in this century – on earth and beyond*.[84]

We have come a long way since the visionary of Patmos sat down in his island prison, gazed through the mists of his own mysterious consciousness, and set down what he saw. If we repudiate the dangerous hijacking of Revelation by the ideologues of the Religious Right, how might we ourselves read it with profit? An obvious but uninteresting way is to see the text as a veiled and coded response to the persecution of the Church, and the increasing corruption of the Roman Empire, in the reign of Domitian. I prefer to sever John's visions from any specific historic context and see them as the horrifying imprint of human brutality on the unconscious mind of a man of profound imaginative capacity: and from that unconscious was projected a language of symbols and archetypes that captured the enduring tragedy of the human condition. It may be that from the vantage point of future historians – if there is enough of a future to engender historians – the condition of the middle classes in Europe during the second half of the twentieth century will be seen as a freakishly tranquil interlude in humanity's incessant war with itself, described by Thomas Hobbes like this: 'Warre, where every man is Enemy to every man . . . in such condition . . . there is no knowledge of the face of the Earth; no account of Time; no Arts; no Letters; no Society; and which is worst of all, continuall feare, and danger of violent death; and the life of man, solitary, poore, nasty, brutish, and short.'[85] Like Hobbes, the author of Revelation is not predicting what might come to pass in the future, he is describing what is already here. He has slashed his brushstrokes onto the canvas and given humanity a picture of itself.

Revelation [6:1] Then I saw the Lamb open one of the seven seals, and I heard one of the four living creatures call out, as with a voice of thunder, 'Come!' [2] I looked, and there was a white horse! Its rider had a bow; a crown was given to him, and he came out conquering and to conquer.

[3] When he opened the second seal, I heard the second living creature call out, 'Come!' [4] And out came another horse, bright red; its rider was permitted to take peace from the earth, so that people would slaughter one another; and he was given a great sword.

[5] When he opened the third seal, I heard the third living creature call out, 'Come!' I looked, and there was a black horse! Its rider held a pair of scales in his hand, [6] and I heard what seemed to be a voice in the midst of the four living creatures saying, 'A quart of wheat for a day's pay, and three quarts of barley for a day's pay, but do not damage the olive oil and the wine!'

[7] When he opened the fourth seal, I heard the voice of the fourth living creature call out, 'Come!' [8] I looked and there was a pale green horse! Its rider's name was Death, and Hades followed with him; they were given authority over a fourth of the earth, to kill with sword, famine, and pestilence, and by the wild animals of the earth.

The grimness of that vision can be a stimulus to action. It can provoke us to a different kind of eschatology than that of the Christian Right; an eschatology not of disaster, but of rescue; an eschatology not of destroying, but of renewing the earth. This is a challenge that runs like a thread through the Hebrew and Christian scriptures. It is why the Bible remains one of the great revolutionary texts of human history. And it is why its first and last word is hope. 'Let the reader understand.'[86]

NOTES

1 Matthew Tindal, *Christianity as Old as the Creation* (1733), quoted in Roy Porter, *Enlightenment* (London: Allen Lane, Penguin Press, 2000), p. 113.

2 Lucidly described in Josh Cohen, *How to Read Freud* (Granta Books, 2005), p. 61.

3 Norman MacCaig, *Collected Poems* (Chatto and Windus, 1990), p. 364.

4 John 1:11.

5 Romans 11:11–27.

6 Robert Alter, *The Five Books of Moses* (Norton, 2004), p. 10.

7 Ibid., p. 11.

8 John Bowker, *The Complete Bible Handbook* (London and New York: Dorling Kindersley, 1998), p. 22.

9 Raymond E. Brown, *An Introduction to the New Testament* (Doubleday, 1996), p. 694.

10 John 14:6.

11 John 14:9; 10:30; 8:58.

12 Robert Funk et al., *The Five Gospels*, p. 36.

13 John 1:18.

14 John Dominic Crossan, *The Birth of Christianity* (HarperSanFrancisco, 1999), p. 486.

15 Papal Bull, *Ineffabilis Deus*, Rome, 8 December 1854.

16 The case for understanding John Paul II as more a Marian than a Christian is made in John Cornwell's *The Pope in Winter: The Dark Face of John Paul II's Papacy* (London: Viking, 2004).

17 One of the most readable versions of the radical position is Thomas L. Thompson's *The Bible in History: How Writers Create a Past* (London: Jonathan Cape, 1999). Thompson believes that we

are just wasting our time if we try to read the Bible as history, and therefore miss the real point of it.

18 An analogy would be the Arthurian legends that surround the resistance of the Britons to the Saxon invasion of the fifth century CE.

19 Ruth Whitman, *An Anthology of Modern Yiddish Poetry* (October House, 1966), reprinted by the Workmen's Circle in 1979.

20 John Gray, *Straw Dogs* (London: Granta, 2003), p. 56.

21 Alter, op. cit., p. 321.

22 Ibid., p. 300.

23 David Grossman, *Revelations* (Canongate, 2005), p. 60.

24 From a poem by Kadya Molodovsky, translated from the Yiddish by Irving Howe, *The Penguin Book of Yiddish Verse*, 1987.

25 Matthew 18:23–34. Incidentally, this parable is coloured pink in the Jesus Seminar translation, meaning that Jesus probably said something like this.

26 Alter, op. cit., p. 879.

27 II Kings 22:8ff.

28 Friedrich Nietzsche, *On the Genealogy of Morals*, 10, trans. by Walter Kaufmann, in *Basic Writings of Nietzsche* (New York: Modern Library, 1992), p. 472.

29 Richard Rorty, *Philosophy and Social Hope* (London: Penguin, 1999), p. 84.

30 I Kings 1, 2.

31 II Kings 17.

32 II Kings 17.

33 Exodus 32.

34 André Schwarz-Bart, *The Last of the Just* (London: Penguin, 1977), p. 383.

35 An interview quoted in *The Portable Hannah Arendt* (New York: Penguin, 2000), p. 17.

36 John 11:50.

37 Article by Hugh S. Pyper on Job in *The Oxford Companion to Christian Thought* (OUP, 2000), p. 347.

38 Letter No. 45, to George and Tom Keats.

39 Extract from chapter 2 in *The Infancy Gospel of Thomas 2:1–7* cited from *The Complete Gospels* (HarperSanFrancisco, 1995), p. 371.

40 Ibid., pp. 371, 381.

41 Luke 1:32–3.

42 Ibid., 24:25–7.

43 Mark 1:9–11.

44 Matthew 1:18–25; Luke 1:26–38; 2:1–7.

45 John 1:1–14.

46 Robert Funk et al., *The Acts of Jesus*, p. 509.

47 Brown, op. cit., p. 176.

48 Exodus 19ff.

49 Incidentally, Luke's version of the sermon is delivered not on a mountain, but on a plain: Luke 6ff.

50 Robert Funk et al., *The Fire Gospels*, pp. 138–59.

51 See, for instance, Matthew 5:36ff, 43ff.

52 Robert Funk et al., *The Five Gospels*, p. 140.

53 I am assuming here that Luke's version of the first beatitude, *Blessed are you who are poor*, is more authentic than Matthew's *Blessed are the poor in spirit* (Luke 6:20; Matthew 5:3).

54 Friedrich Nietzsche, *The Antichrist*, trans. by Walter Kaufmann, *The Portable Nietzsche* (New York: Penguin, 1968), p. 601.

55 Ibid., see footnote on p. 601.

56 Friedrich Nietzsche, *Beyond Good and Evil*, trans. by Kaufmann, *Basic Writings of Nietzsche*, p. 392.

57 Simone Weil, *The Iliad or the Poem of Force* (Peter Lang Inc., 2005).

58 John Dominic Crossan, *The Historical Jesus* (HarperCollins, 1993), p. 273.

59 Crossan, *The Essential Jesus* (HarperSanFrancisco, 1995), pp. 26, 30, 51, 123.

60 Luke 15:11ff.

61 Robert Funk, *Honest to Jesus*, p. 174.

62 Mark 11:15–17; Matthew 21:12, 13; Luke 19:45, 46; John 2:13–17.

63 Numbers [18:1] The Lord said to Aaron: You and your sons and your ancestral house with you shall bear responsibility for offences connected with the sanctuary, while you and your sons alone shall bear responsibility for offences connected with the priesthood. [2] So bring with you also your brothers of the tribe of Levi, your ancestral tribe, in order that they may be joined to you, and serve you while you and your sons with you are in front of the tent of

the covenant. [3] They shall perform duties for you and for the whole tent. But they must not approach either the utensils of the sanctuary or the altar, otherwise both they and you will die. [4] They are attached to you in order to perform the duties of the tent of meeting, for all the service of the tent; no outsider shall approach you. [5] You yourselves shall perform the duties of the sanctuary and the duties of the altar, so that wrath may never again come upon the Israelites. [6] It is I who now take your brother Levites from among the Israelites; they are now yours as a gift, dedicated to the Lord, to perform the service of the tent of meeting. [7] But you and your sons with you shall diligently perform your priestly duties in all that concerns the altar and the area behind the curtain. I give your priesthood as a gift; any outsider who approaches shall be put to death.

64 Robert Funk, *Honest to Jesus*, p. 174.

65 Robert Funk et al., *The Acts of Jesus*, p. 210.

66 The books of Ezra and Nehemiah provide an official version of this history.

67 Luke 6:36.

68 Friedrich Nietzsche, 'The Dawn' trans. by Kaufmann, *The Portable Nietzsche*, pp. 76ff.

69 Acts 22:3; 16:37; 25:12; 18:3; I Thessalonians 2:9; I Corinthians 9:3–18.

70 Galatians 1:13, 14.

71 Romans 7:15.

72 Mark 2:27.

73 Romans 6:1.

74 I Thessalonians 1:10; 5:1–11; I Corinthians 15:35–57; Philippians 3:21.

75 Romans 5:9–10.

76 Acts of the Apostles 21–8.

77 Revelation 1:9.

78 Revelation 1:9, 10.

79 There's a good discussion of the phenomenon in Crossan's *The Historical Jesus*, pp. 104ff.

80 Albert Schweitzer, *The Quest of the Historical Jesus* (London: SCM, 1981), pp. 368–9.

81 Mark 15:34.
82 Revelation [16:16] *And they assembled them at the place that in Hebrew is called Harmagedon.*
83 Quoted in *Sojourners Magazine*, September 2001.
84 Martin Rees, *Our Final Century* (London: William Heinemann, 2003).
85 Thomas Hobbes, *Leviathan* (London: Penguin Classics, 1968), p. 186.
86 Mark 13:14.

CHRONOLOGY

The chronology of the events recounted in the Hebrew Bible is notoriously difficult to compute. A number of factors contribute to the difficulty. The first is the absence in the ancient world of any universally recognized chronological method. One method of establishing a date in the Bible would be to compare it to events outside Israel known to us from other sources, but these are few and far between. The third factor is the use theologically motivated editors made of history, including chronology. It is only from the ninth century BCE, when events in the Bible can be compared with the more detailed and accurate Assyrian and Persian chronologies, that we can speak with any accuracy.

Moses and the Exodus: The date of the Exodus, supposing it to be a historical rather than a mythical event, is much debated. I Kings 6:1 tells us: 'In the four hundredth and eightieth year after the Israelites came out of the land of Egypt, in the fourth year of Solomon's reign . . .' Bearing in mind the reservations expressed above, scholars have linked the date of the Exodus either to the expulsion of the Hyksos kings from Egypt about 1550 BCE or, the more likely date, to the reign of Rameses II in the thirteenth century BCE.

Joshua and the conquest of Palestine: Dating the conquest of Palestine by the Israelites is as uncertain as dating the Exodus. Though the saga is recounted in the Book of Joshua, and some of its sources may date from the ninth century BCE, the book is not reckoned to have reached its present form until the sixth century BCE or later, so we are again gazing through a thick historical mist. If we base ourselves loosely on the Bible's own chronological claims, and assume a historical basis for the account of the forty years spent in the wilderness before the assault on Palestine, then we get a date about either 1440 BCE or 1240 BCE.

The united monarchy: we are on firmer ground by this time and can offer the following approximate dates.

    Saul 1020–1000 BCE

    David 1000–961 (or 965) BCE

    Solomon 961–922 (or 931) BCE

The divided kingdom: 922–721 BCE the kingdom divides into Israel in the north and Judah in the south.

Fall of Israel, the northern kingdom: approximately 721 BCE.

Fall of Judah, the southern kingdom, destruction of the Temple in Jerusalem: approximately 597 BCE.

The exile in Babylon: approximately 597–538 BCE.

Return from exile: 538 BCE.

Building of second Temple in Jerusalem: approximately 520 BCE.

The Greek Empire to the coming of the Romans: 336–63 BCE.

Alexander conquers Israel: 332 BCE.

Alexander dies: 322 BCE.

Palestine taken by Ptolemy: 301 BCE.

Septuagint written in Alexandria: 200 BCE.

Syrian-based Seleucids take Palestine over from Ptolemaic rule: 198 BCE.

Syria becomes a Roman province: 65 BCE.

Roman conquest of Judea: 63 BCE.

Herod the Great, client King under the Romans: 37–4 BCE.

Birth of Jesus: 4 BCE.

Crucifixion of Jesus: some time in the early 30s CE.

Death of Paul according to legend: 65 CE.

Jewish revolt against Romans: 66–70 CE.

Destruction of second Temple by Titus: 70 CE.

BIBLIOGRAPHY

Overview

For a single volume overview that is both popular and scholarly it would be hard to beat *The Complete Bible Handbook* by John Bowker, sumptuously published by Dorling Kindersley in 1998. Among its many virtues is one of the most complete bibliographies on biblical studies available anywhere, listing about one thousand volumes.

Commentaries

The most standard tool for students of the Bible is the commentary, whether of a single book or of the complete works. These come either in a long series or in one or two volumes.

Among the great commentary series are the:

Anchor Bible Commentaries
Cambridge Bible Commentary
Expositor's Bible Commentary
Interpreter's Bible
Jewish Publication Society Torah Commentary
Oxford Bible Commentary.

Among the one- or two-volume commentaries are:
The New Jerome Bible Commentary (Geoffrey Chapman, 1989)
The Books of the Bible, by B. W. Anderson

The Five Books of Moses, by Robert Alter (W. W. Norton & Company, 2004).

General

On topics covered in this book are:

Poet and Peasant, by K. E. Bailey (Eerdmans, 1976)

Through Peasant Eyes, by K. E. Bailey (Eerdmans, 1980)

Escaping from Fundamentalism, by J. Barr (SCM, 1984)

The Garden of Eden and the Hope of Immortality, by J. Barr (SCM, 1992)

Paul: An Introduction to His Thought, by C. K. Barrett (Chapman, 1994)

Jesus: A New Vision, by M. J. Borg (HarperSanFrancisco, 1993)

Problems of Suffering in Religions of the World, by J. W. Bowker (CUP, 1990)

When Time Shall Be No More, by P. Boyer (1992)

The Birth of the Messiah, by R. E. Brown (Doubleday, 1993)

An Introduction to the New Testament, by R. E. Brown (Doubleday, 1997)

Theology of the Old Testament, by W. Brueggemann (Fortress, 1997)

The Pursuit of the Millennium, by N. Cohn (1957)

The Essential Jesus, by John Dominic Crossan (HarperSanFrancisco, 1995)

The Historical Jesus, by John Dominic Crossan (HarperCollins, 1992)

The Birth of Christianity, by John Dominic Crossan (HarperSanFrancisco, 1998)

The Prophets, by A. J. Heschel (The Jewish Publication Society, 1962)

A World Full of Gods, by Keith Hopkins (Weidenfeld &

Nicolson, 1999)

Answer to Job, by C. G. Jung (Meridien, 1960)

Judaism, by Hans Küng (SCM, 1992)

Christianity, by Hans Küng (SCM, 1995)

The Birth of the New Testament, by C. F. D. Moule (A&C Black, 1981)

The Historical Figure of Jesus, by E. P. Sanders (Penguin, 1993)

Paul, the Law and the Jewish People, by E. P. Sanders (Fortress, 1983)

The Bible in History, by Thomas L. Thompson (Jonathan Cape, 1999)

Jesus the Jew, by G. Vermes (Collins, 1973)

Jesus, by A. N. Wilson (1992)

Paul, by A. N. Wilson (1997).

Jesus Seminar

For those who want to take a closer look:

The Complete Gospels, ed. Robert J. Miller (HarperSanFrancisco, 1994)

The Five Gospels: The Search for the Authentic Words of Jesus, by Robert W. Funk, Roy W. Hoover and the Jesus Seminar (Scribner, New York 1993)

The Acts of Jesus: What Did Jesus Really Do?, by Robert W. Funk and the Jesus Seminar (HarperSanFrancisco, 1998)

Honest to Jesus: Jesus for a New Millennium, by Robert W. Funk (HarperSanFrancisco, 1996)

and many others published by the Jesus Seminar's own house, Polebridge Press, Santa Rosa, California.

INDEX